HIGHER EDUCATION SYSTEMS REDESIGNED

SUNY SERIES, CRITICAL ISSUES IN HIGHER EDUCATION
Jason E. Lane and D. Bruce Johnstone, editors

Also in this series
Universities and Colleges as Economic Drivers
edited by Jason E. Lane and D. Bruce Johnstone

Higher Education Systems 3.0
edited by Jason E. Lane and D. Bruce Johnstone

Building a Smarter University
edited by Jason E. Lane

Higher Education Reconsidered
edited by Jason E. Lane

Higher Education Systems Redesigned

FROM PERPETUATION TO INNOVATION TO STUDENT SUCCESS

Edited by
Jonathan S. Gagliardi and Jason E. Lane

With a Foreword by Art Seavey
and a preface by Nancy L. Zimpher

PRESS

Published by State University of New York Press, Albany

For information, contact State University of New York Press, Albany, NY
www.sunypress.edu

Library of Congress Cataloging-in-Publication Data

Names: Lane, Jason E., editor. | Gagliardi, Jonathan S., editor.
Title: Higher education systems redesigned : from perpetuation to
  innovation to student success / edited by Jonathan S. Gagliardi and
  Jason E. Lane ; with a foreword by Art Seavey and a preface by Nancy L.
  Zimpher.
Description: Albany : SUNY Press, 2022. | Series: SUNY series, critical
  issues in higher education | Includes bibliographical references and index.
Identifiers: LCCN 2021054851 (print) | LCCN 2021054852 (ebook) | ISBN
  9781438487670 (hardcover : alk. paper) | ISBN 9781438487694 (ebook) |
  ISBN 9781438487687 (pbk. : alk paper)
Subjects: LCSH: Education, Higher—Aims and objectives—United States. |
  Educational change—United States. | Instructional systems—United
  States—Design. | Academic achievement—United States. | Universities
  and colleges—United States—Administration.
Classification: LCC LA227.4 .H5418 2022 (print) | LCC LA227.4 (ebook) |
  DDC 378.1/010973—dc23/eng/20211203
LC record available at https://lccn.loc.gov/2021054851
LC ebook record available at https://lccn.loc.gov/2021054852

10 9 8 7 6 5 4 3 2 1

Dedicated to the countless staff of system administration offices
across the nation who work tirelessly
to advance systemness and improve student success

CONTENTS

ILLUSTRATIONS

TABLES

FIGURES

FOREWORD

Astronaut, soccer player, news anchor. These were some of my childhood aspirations. State university system bureaucrat certainly did not make the short list. Even as an undergraduate at Georgia Institute of Technology, I could not wrap my head around the role of the fancy-sounding "Board of Regents." I did know they were the ones responsible for increasing my tuition each year.

The purpose and workings of these superstructures, to borrow a word from the editors, can be opaque to the public, to students, to faculty and staff at the institutions under their governance, as well as to the legislators and executives overseeing them. Even when recognized, it's only perhaps in a negative frame: resources that could have gone to campuses, redundancy, or meddling.

Yet, as Lane and Johnstone's (2013) *Higher Education Systems 3.0* presented, and as this follow-up volume of case studies brings to life, I believe state university systems are imperative for our country to thrive. Without them, we risk optimizing for individual institutional interests alone, which, even when viewed collectively across a region or state, can leave whole swaths of students on the periphery, without options for them to better their future.

What I have experienced, and is evident in this collection, is that behind today's most promising work in higher education there is a selfless band of silent innovators. They keep students' and society's interests at the forefront of decision-making, understanding that technical and moral balancing are required. They are creating the strategies and methods as they go, without much precedent on which to rely to guide the way.

The work of *Higher Education Systems Redesigned* marks an important step in beginning to capture these efforts as they unfold, providing for others the inspiration, methods, and lessons on which to improve. "Unfold" is the operative word in this case. The efforts that these contributing authors are undertaking are not short-term plays but will have lasting impact in their states, and hopefully beyond. Investing in this type of work and learning from this great group of leaders makes the job of a program officer at the Bill & Melinda Gates Foundation so rewarding.

I might be a little biased, having spent two formative years working as Director of Policy and Partnership Development for the University System of Georgia. It was there where I first met many of the contributors. That role was an important time of learning and provided a rare convergence of amazing colleagues and conditions ripe for entrepreneurial change.

Each of us faced a similar set of challenges and opportunities from similar vantage points. We were within superstructures responsible for the outcomes of hundreds of thousands of students, yet we could not actually educate students. Instead, we set agendas; provided resources and support; and yes, engaged in compliance activities with institutions, the places where the students actually learn. At the same time, when each one of us looked up, or more accurately, typically toward a dome a few blocks away, we would find our own supervisors—the legislators, the governor, and state actors. It is a lonely place to find yourself in between these very different cultures. So, we often turned across state lines. We discussed, shared ideas, made visits, and occasionally formed a support group.

In this middle role, we were looking outward to a set of institutions and regions, stark differences in their own capacity and resources, and looking down the street to those demanding progress. We had to play interpreter, not just to deliver messages back and forth but to interpret all the voices coming together at once and make sense of a workable vision for the future. Practically, it comes down to something fairly simple in concept: figure out what a collection of institutions working at their best can achieve together, and diplomatically facilitate a set of organizations with budgets totaling in the billions in that direction. Easy, right? I believe this process is the essence of "systemness" that the editors and contributors explore.

People were thinking about systems long before, and some even achieved policy-engineering feats, such as the often-referenced

California Master Plan in 1960. This time is different. A renewed sense of mission and constraints of a country emerging from a recession greatly magnifies the opportunity to think in a new way about what it means to work as a system. There is unprecedented demand for higher education, while political and economic conditions strip our ability to continue serving students with the same methods. Improved data systems and the insights that come from them make it impossible for anyone to ignore what had been inklings about subpar performance with students—especially low-income students, first-generation students, and students of color, those our missions purport we serve. Governors continue to step up and demand "completion," and not without controversy because of the conflict of values some see it as representing with academia. The story is indeed still unfolding.

From Georgia, I was afforded the opportunity to take the position of program officer with the Bill & Melinda Gates Foundation. There, I would have the privilege to get to know the editors of this volume, work with the contributors in a different capacity, and muster substantial resources to invest in people working at the forefront of this growing notion of systemness. When I arrived at the foundation in 2013, our postsecondary success group was in a time of reorganization and refocusing. We had a relatively new leader in Dr. Daniel Greenstein. He himself came from one of these strange superstructures, the University of California, albeit atypical as systems go. It was clear Dan saw great potential in the scale and positioning of university systems as well.

Although we as a foundation had supported work with systems in the past, there was little in the way of a deliberate strategy that would define a role for them in this new operating environment and guide how we should invest. We decided to take a step back. Toward the end of 2013 we solicited letters of interest in an open call, nationally searching for co-creation partners (a fancy phrase with which foundations, and I myself, are enamored and overuse) to help us understand the state of the art for systems. Poring through more than 40 responses, we were amazed at the enthusiasm, the advanced stage of work, and the ambition signaled, especially with such a narrow topic. As my deputy director Suzanne Walsh likes to say, we like to "discover" things in the foundation world like Columbus "discovered" America. In the case of systemness, however, *re*discovery and elevation for others are important roles for the foundation.

We chose to work with 12 partners over a year-long effort. In addition to those represented in this volume, we decided to support and learn from systems in Montana, Wisconsin, Utah, Minnesota, North Carolina, and Hawaii. We gathered virtually several times and once together in person. Aptly enough, it happened to be in Washington, DC, in the back room of a hotel-restaurant that at one time housed the headquarters for the Pony Express. There's a lesson to be drawn from having a discussion about transformation of an industry that is nearly half a millennium old inside a building that now, only through footnote, pays homage to its defunct and irrelevant prior tenant. It is not the lesson you might expect.

These state university system leaders could dig in their heels. They could deny change is coming. They could blame others. They could lament a bygone era. Or you might imagine if you were in their shoes and got over all that, you would figure out a new and innovative way to preserve your core business, making enough incremental changes to stave off the same fate, at least for a short period.

These individuals did not. They reacted with optimism. They had already been hard at work for many years. They do not have to worry about becoming irrelevant because they see their core business as learning and equity of opportunity, not overseeing institutions. By virtue of their vantage point in the middle, by virtue of not being beholden to a single set of interests but charged with interpreting many, by virtue of looking across a set of institutions as labs, much in the way we can look across the states, transformation is not a grieving process for them. They are ready and savvy and know it is their job.

I stated that these leaders are part of a selfless band of silent innovators. You have to be to work effectively in their role. A state system is not the place for glory as an astronaut, soccer player, or talking head of a bygone news era might relish. It is precisely this all guts, no glory role that positions them to conceive of and bring along others to a vision of higher education that focuses on the student. I am grateful to my own band that taught me so much while in Georgia, Vice Chancellors Lynne Weisenbach and Linda Noble; Chief Academic Officer Houston Davis; and his predecessor, David

Morgan. The hours we spent cooped up in conference rooms, on the phone with colleagues across state lines, or traveling together to one of the then 35 institutions in the system, were many, but they forever shaped my own thinking.

My hope is that as you read the stories of others in this role who in *Higher Education Systems Redesigned* are sharing their experiences, you think about the group of people no doubt working with them, their vantage point in the middle, and not just what they are trying to achieve but how they are achieving it as well. We need to work on the silent part, to help others understand this work and ultimately make it better. I am thankful to the editors of this volume for starting this task.

These student-less, seemingly opaque superstructures help to create the balance we need to steward resources while serving all students, especially those who are most disadvantaged. Without state systems, and without nurturing these silent innovators, especially within today's environment of constraints, we stand little chance at delivering on the dramatic improvements needed in equity, economic development, and democracy.

Art Seavey
Former Senior Program Officer
Bill & Melinda Gates Foundation

REFERENCE

Lane, J. E., & Johnstone, D. B. (eds.). (2013). *Higher education systems 3.0: Harnessing systemness, delivering performance.* State University of New York Press.

PREFACE

When I arrived at the State University of New York in 2009 as the system's new chancellor, I realized something immediately. I thought systems were just that—systems. But it became increasingly clear that SUNY—its structure, size, and scope—presented a truly unique opportunity. And in that uniqueness I recognized a special kind of power.

In taking on leadership as SUNY's chancellor, I suddenly had the broad reach of an entire system before me: 64 institutions, 465,000 students, and 88,000 faculty and staff. Woven through the state's 55,000 square miles and 10 varied regions was this richly comprehensive system of community colleges, research universities, liberal arts and technical colleges, health science centers, and research foundations shaping their communities and driving the economy. I have often said that to look at a map of New York is to look at a map of SUNY. We are everywhere. There is really nothing else like it in the country.

Most anyone perusing this book would not be surprised to read that over the last 30 years the United States' global rank in terms of educational attainment of its adult population has fallen dramatically. Where for a long time we were first in the world in educational attainment, we are now, by at least one estimate, twelfth, and in other rankings we are even lower down the list (Alden & Strauss, 2016; Ranking America, 2015). "Leaking education pipelines" in every state have been deemed the primary culprit for the fall-off. But to solve the problem, to seal the leaks, to lift up educational attainment to the level of a great society, it is not enough to identify the problem. We need to find the cause of the corrosion in order to stop it and patch the pipeline once and for all.

To do that, higher education needs to dig deep. As a sector we need to commit to the fact that education is a lifelong continuum, and that what happens in K–12 classrooms is as much our responsibility as what happens once students are on our campuses. If higher education is the sector charged with preparing adults for work and life, we need to be active in ensuring students come to us ready to learn. Working in silos clearly hasn't helped. We need to be one pipeline.

Over the course of the last few decades we have come to understand better than ever before the importance of reliable continuity of high-quality education. We now know that cognitive and social development in the first five years of a child's life is critical in setting their path into adulthood. What happens between birth and five doesn't stay between birth and five. We know that if you enter kindergarten with certain skills sets you have the best chance of being able to do fourth-grade math and reading, and that if you're on track with fourth-grade math and reading, you are more likely to graduate high school on time. If you graduate high school on time, it dramatically helps your chances of enrolling in college, staying in college, and graduating with the skills that empower you to succeed.

These markers are, of course, not assurances of success. Stumbling blocks abound at every stage. Students who live in poor communities face the most daunting challenges, and their chances of success are always gravely under threat. With 22 percent of America's youth living in poverty and millions more on poverty's edge, I argue that it is our collective moral obligation to build an education system that supports these and all students. An educated citizenry is a healthier, safer citizenry. Higher levels of education attainment correlate directly with lower violent crime rates and higher voter turnout and community volunteerism—in short, the hallmarks of the kind of society our collective future depends on.

In the eight years that I served as SUNY's chancellor the system developed a new sense of self that has changed the way the university works. We forced this necessary change in order to maximize our effectiveness as both a quality-of-life and economic driver. In my first 100 days on the job, I traveled the state and visited every one of our campuses—something that had not been done by any of the system's previous 11 chancellors. And in that trip, that crisscrossing of the state in which I came to know the lay of the land, I also came to firmly believe that the best future for public higher education in New York lay in SUNY developing its systemness.

Systemness. I was not even sure it was a word when it came into my mind, but I knew I was on to something. When we at SUNY put our heads together we thought if we enhanced our systemness—our shared capabilities and functionality—how much better could we do in serving students and our communities? What more did SUNY need to do as a system so we could expand access, enhance quality, and improve completion numbers like never before, ultimately setting up students to succeed like never before?

I knew from those first 100 days that figuring out new ways to function as a more efficient, more broad- and deep-thinking system was the answer. And so that is where we put our efforts. In seven years, together with our campuses and governance organizations, we have developed and implemented history-making seamless transfer policy and pathways. We created the most comprehensive student financial literacy tools. We created shared-services policies to save money, and then put those savings right back into the campuses and student services. We created a New York State Cradle to Career Partnership to build the necessary bridges between higher education and K–12. All of this, always, with the intensely focused goal of educating more people and educating them better.

And SUNY is not alone in this effort. It is but one of dozens of systems across the United States. These systems can vary significantly in terms of size, scope, and scale, but they all present a similar opportunity to leverage the collective assets of more than one institution to positively affect the lives of the people they serve and to finally move the needle on the nation's college completion rates.

This volume is a contribution toward this newly invigorated and expanded systemness-minded effort. The authors of the chapters, each accomplished system leaders, offer insights and practical examples from their work, demonstrating how they are improving their own systems and the students they serve.

Excellence is always the goal. Pushing every day to figure out what works best in elevating educational attainment levels to where we have our best shot at creating a society in which everyone has the chance to succeed. We can't guarantee success for everyone, but together we can make sure everyone has the *chance*.

Nancy L. Zimpher
Co-founder of StriveTogether
Senior Fellow, National Association of System Heads
Chancellor Emeritus of the State University of New York

REFERENCES

Alden, E., & Strauss, R. (2016). *How America stacks up: Economic competitiveness and U.S. policy.* Council on Foreign Relations Press.

Ranking America. (2015). https://rankingamerica.wordpress.com/category/education/

ACKNOWLEDGMENTS

The SUNY series Critical Issues in Higher Education was developed to bring together thought leaders to explore an issue of critical important to the future of public higher education. This volume explores the role of higher education systems in advancing student success. Chapters included here were written by experts in the fields—the individuals who led system-level efforts that were directly focused on advancing student learning and increasing completion rates. Over the long term, some of these efforts have declined while others have soared. Collectively, they represent early efforts of *systemness*—and have been followed by dozens of like-minded efforts across the country.

We are indebted to many folks for their contributions—thoughts, suggestions, and support in developing this volume—a volume that has taken many years to come to fruition. The contributors of this volume have been incredibly patient, many transitioning roles since the idea first germinated. We thank them for sharing their experiences and insights. Rebecca Martin, Executive Director of the National Association of System Heads (NASH), provided significant encouragement to bring the volume to fruition, in addition to contributing a chapter. Nancy Zimpher, Chancellor Emeritus of the SUNY System and a senior fellow of NASH, first advanced the concept of *systemness* and has encouraged us to examine the concept in action in other systems. As always, the team at SUNY Press has been great to work with—and special thanks go to Beth Bouloukos (who started this journey with us), Rebecca Colesworthy (who finished the journey with us), and Ryan Morris for shepherding the Critical Issues book series and this volume.

This book is dedicated to our friends, colleagues, and others who have advanced systemness in various forms and fashions over the last decade. We have learned much from all of you and know that your tireless efforts are working to change higher education for the better.

Jonathan S. Gagliardi and Jason E. Lane

Part I

BACKGROUND

1

THE EVOLUTION OF HIGHER EDUCATION SYSTEMS FROM REGULATORS TO FACILITATORS TO LEADERS OF STUDENT SUCCESS

JONATHAN S. GAGLIARDI AND
JASON E. LANE

ABSTRACT

Long an afterthought of the American higher education ecosystem, multicampus systems are now more important than ever. These entities have the unique ability to harness the collective capacity of their constituent campuses to address some of the most pressing issues facing the United States by scaling out best practices, leveraging data and analytics, and creating platforms that optimize and personalize the higher education experience for increasingly diverse students. This focus on *systemness*, fueled by the complementary yet distinct roles of systems and campuses, has led to a series of breakthroughs that could finally move the dial on access and completion rates and position the United States once again as first in the world in educational attainment, social mobility, and economic growth.

Higher education systems are aspiring to be more than the sum of their parts. The transformative change efforts of higher education systems have focused largely on flipping the paradigm of scale in a manner that enhances their campuses and the educational experiences of their students. Broadly speaking, systems are seeking to move beyond the *isolated* impact of campus efforts to encourage and support a *collective* impact approach that supports and facilitates meaningful and purposeful collaboration between faculty, staff, and leaders across campuses (Lane & Johnstone, 2013). Rather than perpetuating the traditional structural and cultural forms of higher education as we have come to know them, some systems are taking measures to reconfigure campus interactions in ways that meet the current and emerging needs of people, communities, and economies in the twenty-first century (Gagliardi, 2015).

One area that system leaders are increasingly focusing their efforts on is student success. However, *student success* is not a term traditionally associated with higher education systems. Students attend campuses, not systems. Campuses, not systems, grant degrees. Faculty teach on campuses, not at the system office. Alumni tend to associate with a particular campus, not the system. In their landmark study of higher education systems, Lee and Bowen (1971) found that student issues remained the prerogative of campuses and none of the multicampus system administrations in their study had designated a senior leader with responsibility for student affairs.

Yet, in recent years, a growing number of higher education systems have begun to shift their focus away from historic responsibilities for coordinating, regulating, and allocating financial resources among institutions to harnessing, leveraging, and sharing the collective assets of the campuses on behalf of the students they serve.

This shift is significant in two fundamental ways. First, while institutions have been increasingly focused on student success, it is system leaders that are uniquely situated to understand and respond to the increasing number of students moving between multiple institutions on their way toward a college degree (Lane, 2018; Soares et al., 2017). Second, systems, largely, have been structured to operate like a state agency, insuring that rules and regulations are applied and adhered to. Lee and Bowen (1971) referred to system administration as a "community of bureaucrats." In this new orientation, systems are moving more toward capacity building and facilitation of collaboration, with a focus on supporting academic programming and student success and an acknowledgment of engaging faulty and other stakeholders across the system in these efforts (Lane & Johnstone, 2013).

The ongoing evolution of higher education systems is a central development in US higher education and is the primary focus of this volume. Higher education systems have an integral part to play in improving student outcomes and closing equity gaps. They can be an interface that allows campuses to leverage their collective capacity and a tool for scaling out evidence-based practices. Indeed, higher education systems are increasingly working in collaboration with campuses to ensure quality, and create a more agile public higher education ecosystem by facilitating, incentivizing, and accelerating transformational changes on behalf of students and in line with state and national goals.

Still, a host of challenges confront efforts by higher education systems to spark innovation among and between their campuses. The histories of the relationships between the state and the higher education system, and the system and its individual campuses are often fraught with contention (Johnstone, 2013). Such history can make it difficult to implement a shared vision for the entire system, as well as corresponding goals and strategies. The distinctiveness and autonomy of individual campuses contrasts with the nature of higher education systems to centralize and standardize. Harmonizing these competing organizational facets is no easy task. As demonstrated in the chapters in this volume, these forces have resulted in systems playing a more facilitative leadership role, setting a broad vision and then providing support and structures to facilitate campuses moving in a similar direction, while also being able to honor and utilize their distinctiveness. And not all of these efforts have been successful—yielding their own lessons.

This chapter lays the foundation for the rest of this volume. It begins by describing how the evolution of higher education systems is being pushed by the changing mobility patterns and demographics of modern undergraduates and pulled by increased attention of state and national leaders on the college completion agenda. Following this, the chapter briefly traces the origins of higher education systems in the United States, with particular attention to key evolutions in their structures and functions. Next, the current state of higher education systems is discussed, including an ongoing shift toward prioritizing student success and promoting innovation. This chapter ends by highlighting some of the key contributions of this volume.

THE PUSH AND PULL OF CHANGE

The focus of higher education systems on student success is much more than a rallying cry for change. It is a documented effort by some system governing boards and administrations to adapt policies, resources, technologies, practices, and institutional culture to facilitate greater collaboration among campuses to improve student completion numbers. These efforts range from activities focused on recruitment to retention to completion.

In fact, many state and system leaders have set systemwide goals intended to drive campus-level actions around student completion (Virginia's Community Colleges, n.d.; SUNY, n.d.; California State University, n.d.; Ma & Hartley, 2017):

- Virginia's Community College system committed to tripling completions by 2021.

- California State University System has committed to significantly increasing graduation rates for new and transfer students as well as eliminating all achievement gaps by 2025.

- The State University of New York committed to moving the number of completions each year from 93,000 in 2015 to 150,000 in 2025.

- Utah's Board of Regents adopted a goal of increasing completion in Utah's System of Higher Education to 28 awards (i.e., certificates or degrees) per 100 full-time equivalent students by the year 2025.

The goals themselves are not as important as the fact that such goals are being set by systems. They indicate a clear shift of system leaders toward focusing on student success; moreover, the only way to achieve these goals is for institutions and systems to arrange themselves in more integrated ways in order to collectively facilitate student success. Yet, what is driving this interest in student completion by system leaders?

One of the major pressures pulling systems into this space has been the significant focus of elected leaders, the media, and funders on the "completion crisis"—essentially, the United States is falling behind internationally in terms of the education level of its citizenry. According to the 2019 *Education at a Glance* report (OECD, 2019), the United States ranks eleventh in the proportion of 25–34-year-olds with a postsecondary education credential. Forty years ago, the United States led the world in being the most well-educated country. The national inability to significantly improve access and completion rates (along with the pandemic impact) has exacerbated a workforce gap. Prior to the pandemic, the U. S. was set to have a shortage of about five million college-educated workers by 2020 (Carnevale et al., 2014). That gap has only worsened since the pandemic, with many opting for early retirement or reconsidering employment options; yet the need remains for most workers to have some college.

The fact that so many countries have outpaced the United States' ability to educate a large proportion of our citizens led to several leaders in the public and private sectors calling for reform. In his first State of the Union address, President Obama made it a national goal that "by 2020, America will once again have the highest proportion of college graduates in the world" (CNN, 2010). The Lumina Foundation (n.d.) "committed to increasing the proportion of Americans with high-quality degrees, certificates and other credentials to 60 percent by 2025." And, within two years of Obama's call to increase completion, at least 19 states had established their own goals to meet their contributions to achieve this new national priority and by 2019 nearly every state had set or was considering a state goal of having at least 55 percent of their citizens earn a postsecondary credential by 2025—meaning that governors and other elected state officials began leading some of the most significant reform efforts and necessitating that system leaders follow along (Education Commission of the States, 2017).

These efforts had some effect. The percentage of working adults in the United States with a college degree increased. Between 2008 and 2017, the percentage of 25–65-year-olds with a credential beyond high school increased from 37.9 to 47.6 percent.[1] While progress is good, the country had not reclaimed its position as first in the world in college-educated adults by 2020. It also means that without dramatic progress, the United States will be short of Lumina's 2025 goal (Lumina Foundation, 2019).

There are a number of factors pushing system leaders to support a more collaborative multicampus approach to increasing completion numbers. To be certain, all systems are different in terms of their size, scale, complexity, political environment, financial stability, and governance authority. Yet, many systems are facing diminished or stagnating resources, necessitating new ways to share resources or find greater economies of scale. And there is a growing recognition that limited resources may be better used to scale out evidence-based practices, instead of continuing to fund new, unproven, and isolated projects. The most significant of the push factors are likely the changing demographics and mobility patterns of college students.

Much of the country is anticipating declines in the number of students graduating from high school (with some areas declining by more than 15% by 2028), signaling a shift to more diverse and more nontraditional students (Bransberger & Michaelau, 2016). In fact, the modern undergraduate student population is already incredibly (and increasingly) diverse and contrasts with the description provided by anecdotal wisdom of the "traditional student" being a white, 18–22-year-old, full-time student. In fact, nearly 6 in 10 (58%) undergraduates are now post-traditional learners (Soares et al., 2017). These post-traditional students tend to be older, full-time employed, financially independent, and/or connected to the military. In comparison to other undergraduates, these students are more likely to be women, nonwhite, and to have dependents. Post-traditional learners are also four times more likely than other undergraduates to already have a postsecondary credential, and more than 12 times as likely to live off campus (Soares et al., 2017). The needs of these post-traditional learners differ greatly from the "traditional" undergraduate. This necessitates campuses developing new and different modes for supporting students as they work toward a college degree.

More than more diverse, they are also more mobile. For example, the National Student Clearinghouse found that 38 percent of the 2.8 million students entering college for the first time in fall 2011 transferred to a different institution at least once within six years (Shapiro et al., 2018). Between 2011 and 2017, 47.32 percent of transfer students changed institutions more than once (Shapiro et al., 2018). Within the State University of New York system, nearly half of all baccalaureate graduates attend at least two institutions before completing (Lane, 2018). Moreover, in the process of transferring students lose credit, which can be costly and ultimately lengthen time to degree. According to the Government Accountability Office (GAO 2017), students who transferred from 2004 to 2009 lost an average of 43 percent of their credits. Simply put, the success of modern undergraduates is no longer the domain of an isolated campus; it depends on a more collaborative approach that marries the best of what the nation's diverse colleges and universities have to offer.

WHY SYSTEMS?

The multicampus system is one of the dominant organizational features of US higher education, though they have often been overlooked as a potential leader in improving student success and completion. According to the National Association of System Heads (NASH) there are more than 50 multicampus systems of higher education operating in 37 states.[2] The size and scope of these systems range significantly. For example, the Southern Illinois University has two degree-granting institutions with approximately 20,000 students, while SUNY is comprised of 64 two-year and four-year degree-granting institutions serving nearly 600,000 students in credit-bearing courses. Some states also have more than one system in place. New York, for example, is home to both the City University of New York and the State University of New York. In Texas, there are seven distinct multicampus systems of higher education. Collectively, they have an unprecedented opportunity to affect change.

At the time of this writing, 23 of these systems have joined the Taking Student Success to Scale (TS3) initiative, designed to support systems in implementing evidence-based practices that positively impact retention and completion. In 2014–2015, these systems collectively served 3.1 million undergraduate students, or about 18 percent of the entire undergraduate population in the United States. In that same year, students in this systems earned approximately

530,000 undergraduate degrees and certificates, or about 20 percent of the national number. So, this one network of 23 systems has the potential to reach one in five of every undergraduate student in the US. And this network represents fewer than half of all systems in the US. There are no other structures in the United States that collectively govern so many institutions and oversee the educational opportunities of so many students.

THE ROAD TO SYSTEMS

To understand the current effort to redesign the work of higher education systems, it is important to understand their historical evolution. Public higher education multicampus systems were designed to bring efficiency and effectiveness to the governance of a growing public postsecondary education sector, coordinate access to higher education for the state's citizens, and ensure the alignment of institutions with the needs, goals, and aspirations of the states that created and funded them. With rare exception, such as the creation of the University of the State of New York in 1784,[3] the emergence of public coordination of higher education through centralized governance, multicampus systems did not occur until the late nineteenth century (McGuiness, 2013). However, these entities have important roots that can be traced back to the origins of higher education in the United States.

In the colonial era, colleges existed at the nexus of their respective communities, governments, and religions (McClendon, 2003; Thelin, 2019). Institutions like Harvard, Princeton, and Yale each received land donations and tax levies, among other benefits, from their particular colonies. These institutions represented an early form of public-private partnership, which Thelin (2019) dubbed "state-church colleges" (p. 13) because of the degree to which the colonies and churches exerted control over and provided support to these institutions. In fact, the development of lay governing boards comprised of external stakeholders that have legal authority for the college and, in theory, serve as a buffer and a connection between the outside world and the academic organization remain the dominant governance paradigm for higher education in the United States today.

A major factor during this era was the evolution of the church-state model into what we know today as a clear differentiation between public and private institutions. After the Revolutionary War, state governments (as opposed to the federal government) retained primary authority over the colleges within their borders.[4] State governments sought to exert greater control over the colonial colleges, who resisted believing that they were private institutions that should not fall under direct control of the state. Eventually, the distinction between public and private higher education was outlined by the 1819 US Supreme Court *Dartmouth College v. Woodward* decision, which overturned efforts by the New Hampshire legislature to place Dartmouth College under greater public control. In addition to making the distinction between a public and private institution, the decision also sparked backlash from state legislatures, which quickly went about forming new institutions more directly under their control.

During the early nineteenth century a host of forces converged to tie the states and higher education together more tightly. As the nation's population grew and migrated westward into new territories, the United States experienced significant growth in the number of higher education institutions. For example, from 1800 to 1850 roughly 700 public and private institutions were founded. However, the instability of the era meant that only 250 of those institutions lasted until 1861 (Thelin, 2019). This era was marked by limited coordination in terms of state governance, with historians Brubacher and Rudy (2002, p. 427) arguing that a distinguishing aspect of this era was its "un-systematized diversity."

The growth in the number of institutions and the number of students, as well as the expanding responsibilities of state governments, led many states to explore alternative modes of governance that allowed for what they hoped would be greater coordination among public colleges and universities in terms of the use of state resources, provision of academic programs, and responding to state needs (McGuiness, 2013). At the same time, the strong tradition of having lay governing boards overseeing higher education institutions limited the options available to them. The result in many states was the creation of governing boards that had some level of institutional authority but were responsible for multiple institutions, not just a single campus.

Since their emergence in the late nineteenth century, public higher education multicampus systems have continued to develop and evolve. The move toward centralized governance structures has ebbed and flowed over the last 150 years, but the overall movement has been toward greater coordination, not less. McGuiness (2013) identified six distinct eras of public higher education system evolution, which we list here. To this list we add a description of a new era, one in which the current focus of systems on student success and completion is occurring.

Period 1: Progressive Era (1880s to World War I). Many states moved from isolated governing boards to multicampus governing and coordinating board systems. The intent was to create a structure to govern the growing number of public institutions and associated state investment more efficiently and effectively. An additional effect was to create a buffer between the institutions and the elected officials that allowed for a difference management of the tension between local and regional politics.

Period 2: Consolidation Era (World War I to World War II). The advent of World War I, the Great Depression, and World War II created disruptive social, political, and economic conditions. Many states that did not already have them created statewide governing bodies as a means to insulate public higher education from overt external interference, in particular limiting the extent to which the governor or state legislatures could directly control and impact higher education.

Period 3: Capacity Building, Expansion, and Standardization (World War II to the 1970s). Demand for higher education grew significantly in the aftermath of World War II. States further developed or revised consolidated governance models in response to the massification movement, so as to provide postsecondary learning opportunities that met minimum standards to larger portions of their populations. In addition, the 1965 Higher Education Act required states to identify ways to achieve greater efficiencies in the use of state and federal investments in higher education. By the 1970s nearly every state had some sort of statewide governing or coordinating body, though their powers varied markedly between states.

Period 4: The Rise of Decentralization (1980s). During the 1980s there was pushback against "centralized state control" in many countries and across public sectors. The movement was toward introducing more businesslike principles into government operations. For higher education in some states, this resulted in reconfiguring the governance of higher education toward greater institutional autonomy and flexibility (and, thus, toward more decentralized governance models). This led some states to pass sweeping reforms intended to grant individual campuses more control over key functions (e.g., tuition setting, contracting, human resources). These moves were intended to enhance the capability of public institutions to tailor their offerings to local needs and to manage institutional resources more effectively.

Period 5: Restructuring amid a Changing State Role (1990s–Early 2000s). During this era, some states moved toward more decentralization, while others swung toward more centralization. States began to apportion financial support in more targeted ways, with an emphasis on research and economic development, seeking to invest in higher education in ways that advanced a "public agenda" often directed at the state's long-term economic competitiveness. Previously, state funding was focused on building higher education infrastructure and capacity to meet growing demands for access through general fund appropriations. This era was marked by the emergence of funds tied to specific policy goals and performance.

Period 6: Responses to Recession and Slow Economic Recovery (Early 2000s–Early 2010s). In the wake of the recession of 1999–2001 and the Great Recession of 2008–2010 states intensified their efforts to alter governance structures. Many of the prominent themes of this era centered on cost reductions and efficiencies, such as centralizing back-office functions, reducing duplicative programs and offerings, and creating economies of scale.

Period 7: Collective Impact and Student Success (Early 2010s–Present). In addition to the preceding eras mapped out by McGuiness (2013), we believe that the current era of systems is differentiated from previous eras due to the refocusing of the work of systems away from being simply allocators, regulators, and coordinators to focusing on facilitative leadership that brings campuses together to work on shared problems through the distribution of best practices, processes of co-learning and co-problem-solving, and sharing of resources. The most important shift in this era is a new focus of systems on student success and equity.

In period 7, rather than (or in addition to) system administrations focusing on institutional coordination, there is greater focus on developing policies and practices that support student learning and student success. The result is that there are fewer fights over where authority lies as system administrations focus on cross-cutting issues instead of trying to replicate the responsibilities of campuses (see also chapter 9). The recognition of the complementary yet distinct roles of systems and campuses has been important. It is this shift toward facilitative leadership to drive student success through collective action of campuses that is the focus of this volume and the included case studies.

For example, SUNY recently developed a systemwide seamless transfer policy, intended to allow students to transfer easily among the system's 64 campuses (Lane, 2018). The initiative was driven by an analysis of student mobility data that demonstrated that students move in a multidirectional fashion. As such, the existing policy framework based on unidirectional, upward, vertical articulation agreements needed to be reconfigured to reflect the attendance patterns of students as shown by the data. To do that effectively, a complex negotiation between system leadership, campus administrators, and shared governance groups took place to identify transfer paths based on shared understanding of foundational knowledge while allowing for campus distinctiveness. The focus was on harnessing system resources to meet the demands of increasing student mobility and accelerate time to degree. Supporting multidirectional transfer patterns at both the two-year and four-year levels is the kind of innovative initiative that could only be accomplished by a system.

This volume provides an overview of several initiatives that represent the type of collective impact approach that is discussed in this volume, and they were selected as they were part of a collaborative effort funded by the Bill & Melinda Gates Foundation. What is important to note is that while these particular initiatives had varying levels of sustainability, the systems that birthed them have remained largely committed to advancing student success. So, while projects may ebb and flow, the overall direction of systems appears to remain headed toward increased collaboration to support student success.

REALIGNING HIGHER EDUCATION TOWARD COMPLETION THROUGH SYSTEMS

Higher education systems are useful tools for encouraging colleges and universities to realign from a focus on student access to a focus on student completion. By providing shared services, setting systemwide priorities, driving innovation, and coordinating alternative pathways that include online learning, systems and campuses are leveraging one another in new and exciting ways. The current emphasis on degree attainment has redistributed the responsibility of social mobility and economic growth more equally among research universities, comprehensive institutions, and community colleges. Due to their ability to serve as laboratories for innovation, hubs for analysis, and gatherers of organizational and environmental intelligence, systems are able to advance innovations, create new resource strategies, foster enabling policy environments, and identify economies of scale that may be crucial for addressing the national need for increasing attainment of a high-quality academic credential. The examples from this volume illustrate the vital role that systems play in innovating and scaling, as well as the challenges that lay before those pursuing such a path.

As readers progress through this volume, it is important to view the included case studies through that particular lens. First, a case study is bounded by both space and time (Yin, 2005). The cases included in this volume are snapshots of initiatives from particular systems for a particular period of time. These cases purposefully focus on the early stages of each initiative, so that readers are able to learn from these efforts to design and implement system-level initiatives focused on improving student success. These initiatives continued beyond the duration covered in this volume. Some of them continued to grow, some transformed, some ceased to exist. We have attempted to include the most relevant aspects of the epilogues to these cases in chapters 2 and 9; however, readers will inevitably be aware of developments not included herein. What is important for this volume is to recognize that while not all of the cases may have achieved their original goals, each are early endeavors of systemness that inform our understanding of this work and serve as examples of the type of work that we now see often occurring in multicampus systems across the country.

Second, approaching student success initiatives from a system perspective is very different than analyzing it within a single institution framework. Our intention here is to assess the system dynamics associated with such approaches; however, we do acknowledge that the ultimate impact of each effort takes place on a campus. Lane (2019) has suggested that system initiatives for student success have three key sets of drivers: 1) governing board drivers, 2) system administrative drivers, 3) institutional drivers. The case studies each address these drivers in different ways, though the majority of the focus is on the governing and system administration drivers. That said, within the institutional drivers, it is important to understand the particular nature of the students within that institution. While we do not delve into the decades of research into student development (see Pascarella & Tenerzini, 2005; Mayhew et al., 2016), we acknowledge that the ultimate success of each of these efforts will be their ability to contextualize efforts based on the needs of students and future research will be needed to understand how system-level efforts vary among various student groups.

This volume is based on the idea that the American higher education ecosystem can be more fluid and dynamic in order to better serve contemporary students, and that systems are uniquely poised to facilitate such a transformation. The authors examine their own system-led efforts at creating the structural, policy, and cultural changes that boost student outcomes and close attainment gaps. It is organized into four parts. First, part 1 (chapters 1 and 2) provides an analysis of the factors influencing shifts in higher education systems and a model for intentional innovation in higher education systems. Part 2 (chapters 3–5) of the volume examines system-led efforts at reimagining educational delivery. Part 3 (chapters 6–7) focuses on how systems are building innovative infrastructures, and part 4 (chapters 8 and 9) provides frameworks for designing and implementing large-scale change.

Balancing the need for consensus about what constitutes quality with the reality that decisions around programs and content are best made locally is a theme that emerges throughout this volume. In chapter 3, Audrey Hovanesian of the California State University (CSU) system, and Ken O'Donnell of CSU Dominguez Hills report on the efforts to scale high-impact practices (HIPs). After recognizing the success of a select few campuses in scaling HIPs, CSU used its convening power to establish minimum HIP standards, which led to the creation of a template that campuses could adopt to their local contexts. This eventually led to the placement of HIPs on student transcripts, which led to better data and more rapid cycle innovation and scaling.

In chapter 4, Houston Davis, formerly of the University System of Georgia (now of University of Central Arkansas), and Myk Garn of USG describe how the University System of Georgia sought out ways to preserve academic quality, improve affordability, and shorten time to degree. Through its New Learning Models 2030 Task Force, the USG worked across its 29 institutions to better serve over 300,000 students through a shared focus on meaningful degree opportunities, a focus on providing a better education for at-risk students, and creating new efficiencies through such means as Massive Open Online Courses (MOOCs), open educational resources, reinvented academic and student supports, and more refined assessments brought to bear by data and analytics.

In few places is the use of big data and analytics to drive innovation more apparent than the Tennessee Board of Regents (TBR), which former TBR vice president for academic affairs Tristan Denley (now of the University System of Georgia), writes about in chapter 5. By combining principles of behavioral economics, massive volumes of data and sophisticated analyses, and most importantly, people who care about students, TBR led the creation of a massive analytics infrastructure that has created unprecedented gains in access and completion while making a major dent in equity gaps. Only through careful campus partnerships, vision, and attention to the intended—and unintended—consequences of using big data was TBR able to scale predictive analytics across its campuses. TBR recognized that predictive analytics is not to be used as a replacement for teaching, learning, and advising but rather as a tool to augment the human elements of each of those functions.

These kind of data-driven educational innovations can be difficult to implement. The University of Texas System (UTS) created its Total Education Experience (TEx) to bring transformational models of education that are student focused and industry aligned in such a fashion that creates a more personalized and meaningful education for every student. Steven Mintz, formerly of the University of Texas at Austin, details the opportunities and challenges in transforming curricular design, pedagogy, delivery models, student lifecycle services, and learning analytics in chapter 6.

Cultural divides also appear throughout the volume. The University System of Maryland's (USM) Course Redesign Initiative is an example of how to bridge them. In chapter 7, Jo Boughman and M. J. Bishop of the USM detail how to cultivate and enable a more innovative academic culture. By using complex adaptive systems theory, and generative, unifying, and convergent leadership, the USM created meaningful change that was embraced by its constituent campuses despite facing a host of challenges.

Rebecca Martin of the National Association of System Heads (NASH) and Jason Lane, a former senior leader in the SUNY System (and currently of Miami University in Ohio) (both founding members of the Taking Student Success to Scale (TS3) Steering Committee), use the Collective Impact framework to examine lessons from efforts to leverage networks of systems to affect student success in chapter 8. One key element of this effort is the realization among systems that they must simultaneously facilitate innovation among their campuses while also transforming themselves.

Finally, chapter 9, by Lane and Gagliardi, presents the innovation cube, a framework for understanding and executing large-scale change based on the analysis of the cases included in this volume. We find that focusing on three key aspects (capacity building, strategy and policy, and structure) is important for addressing the challenges and opportunities facing systems and their campuses as they try to reconfigure US higher education in ways that put students first.

IMPLICATIONS FOR SYSTEMS

Given the myriad pressures faced by multicampus systems in a constantly changing environment, the ability to effectively leverage the process of organizational learning is growing in importance. Yet, the internal and external complexities faced by multicampus systems can create barriers to such a process. Competing interests of diverse campuses and academic units—which are largely driven by resource dependency, prestige, and a desire for autonomy—can impede the ability of the multicampus system to learn from its member campuses (Becher & Trowler, 2001; Pfeffer & Salancik, 1978). Consequently, efforts to create shared services, to promote collaborations, and to share best practices among member campuses can be met with resistance to ongoing transformational efforts led by the multicampus system office, limiting their effectiveness. Externally, government and private-sector pressures that include emphasizing metrics and outcomes like the Postsecondary Institutional Ratings System (PIRS)—which eventually became the College Scorecard; an emphasis on aligning educational supply and workforce demands; and performance or incentive funding initiatives that prioritize rapid change are orientations that systems and institutions are unaccustomed to.

The many permutations of multicampus system traits and initiatives lend themselves to a process of change that is evolutionary, not disruptive (Drucker, 1985; Johnson & Rush, 1995; Kirzner, 1973). The combination of internal pressures, external demands, and contrasting organizational cultures results in incremental change that has implications for the process of organizational learning for multicampus systems and their institutions in the following areas:

1. **Scale as an information resource.** The scale of activity in a large system can have a multiplier effect, especially in an era of big data. Systems by definition have access to

information that can serve as a resource for understanding and improvement. What the campus scales up, the system can scale out, thus magnifying impact.

2. **Institutional Diversity allows for incremental and organic innovation.** The variety of institutions that comprise the system can serve as laboratories for innovation and allow small-scale testing of options that can serve the system as a whole.

3. **Structures for the dissemination of knowledge and customized delivery.** The system has established structures to collect and disseminate knowledge about its activities. These can serve to inform institutions and policymakers about the potential of reforms to support articulated goals.

4. **Standardization for efficiency and optimization.** The capacity of the system to identify best practices and minimum standards of quality can lead to greater efficiency and ensure quality. As new ideas emerge and are vetted, they can be quickly implemented as system initiatives, preventing redundant or archaic practices from remaining entrenched. Resulting savings can then be reinvested to support the other three elements.

5. **Creating platforms that the user can shape.** Through collaboration with campuses, the system is ideally situated to identify areas of convergence across multiple campuses, allowing pockets of campuses to work together in pursuit of their most important priorities. This is far different from the heavy-handed and mandate-centric approach systems became known for among campus constituents, which has contributed to lingering ill will that is only now being overcome.

Historically, systems have pulled hard levers, including money and policy, in order to do this. Given the increasing scarcity of resources, and ineffectiveness of broad-brush policies, systems have shifted, pulling soft levers in order to generate buy-in, share ownership, and to defer to local decision-making at the campus level where possible.

These include convening and engaging stakeholders, aligning interests and priorities, promoting best practices, leveraging data, and creating investment and incentive funds. Systems can use their perch to identify service gaps that make it difficult for the contemporary student to earn a credential and reap the full benefits of a higher education.

Furthermore, senior leaders and staff must understand the social, political, and economic environments that have an effect on the value propositions, resource strategies, processes, and revenue formulas that are required of them and their institutions. A deeper understanding of the processes of learning and change can ultimately identify what is scalable and what is not, leading to more flexible and dynamic networked organizations of systems and campuses that can flex to any challenge. This process facilitates innovation by developing a more systemic and comprehensive process for getting the buy-in required for change among key constituents. This information can be used to critically evaluate systems as organizational solutions to a set of problems facing US higher education (such as student completion, global competitiveness, and financial stress).

CONCLUSION

Higher education systems are creating stronger partnerships with their institutions based on community-centered design. Through a focus on better and more integrated data, evidence, and collective impact, higher education systems are advancing student centered and self-managed education; transforming educational delivery and student success; fostering innovative approaches and policies among institutions; building and enhancing a more cohesive infrastructure that promotes diverse pathways toward completion, as well as equitable access and outcomes; and fundamentally creating innovative higher education business models. Systems are becoming more dynamic, serving as interfacing organizations by using the uniqueness of the campuses they govern to offer solutions to the most pressing social and economic challenges of today. Indeed, there are promising signs that a new, more dynamic era of higher education is emerging, however quietly, right under our noses by these silent innovators we know as higher education systems.

CHAPTER 1 TAKEAWAYS

- Higher education multicampus systems are emerging as an important means for advancing student success efforts.

- Significant numbers of students now accumulate credits from multiple institutions before they complete their degree program (if they complete at all).

- Systems call for development of policy and practice based on how students now experience higher education, transcending institutional boundaries.

- Systems are moving beyond traditional roles as regulator, allocator, and coordinator toward more facilitative leadership, working with and across campuses to execute and sustain change.

NOTES

1. Note that beginning in 2014, workforce credentials began to be included in the total of postsecondary credentials.
2. This includes only systems that have system leadership and administration that is distinct from the leadership of a campus. For example, the Pennsylvania State University has 24 campuses throughout the state but is not included in this count as the president of the flagship campus (located in University Park) also serves as the head of network of campuses.
3. USNY is an umbrella licensing and accreditation body created by the state constitution that sets standards for all education programs pre-K through graduate education in New York. It is still in existence at the time of this writing.
4. The omission of any mention of education from the U.S. Constitution and the eventual passage of the 10th Amendment, which reserved all powers not enumerated in the Constitution for state authority, reinforced that higher education was primarily a state issue (Brubacher, 1967; McClendon, 2003; Millard, 1979).

REFERENCES

Becher, T., & Trowler, P. R. (2001). *Academic tribes and territories: Intellectual enquiry and the culture of disciplines* (2nd ed.). Society for Research into Higher Education and Open University Press.

Bransberger, P., & Michaelau, D. K. (2016). *Knocking at the college door: Projections of high school graduates, December 2016.* Western Interstate Commission for Higher Education.

Brubacher, J. S., & Rudy, W. (2002). *Higher education in transition: A history of American colleges and universities* (4th ed.). London: Routledge.

Brubacher, J. S. (1967). The autonomy of the university: How independent is the republic of scholars? *Journal of Higher Education, 38*(5), 237–249.

California State University. (n.d.). Graduation initiative 2025. https://www2.calstate.edu/csu-system/why-the-csu-matters/graduation-initiative-2025. Retrieved September 4, 2021.

Carnevale, A. P., Smith, N., & Strohl, J. (2014). *Recovery: Job growth and education requirements through 2020.* Georgetown Center on Education and the Workforce.

CNN. (2010, January 28). Transcript: Obama's first State of the Union speech. www.cnn.com/2010/POLITICS/01/27/sotu.transcript/index.html

Drucker, P. F. (1985). *Innovation and entrepreneurship: Practices and principles.* Harper & Row.

Education Commission of the States. (2017, October). *Attainment goals and plans.* https://www.ecs.org/wp-content/uploads/Attainment_Goals_and_Plans.pdf

Gagliardi, J. S. (2015). From perpetuation to innovation: Breaking through barriers to change in higher education. In J. E. Lane (Ed.), *Higher education reconsidered: Executing change to drive collective impact* (pp. 61–96). State University of New York Press.

Government Accountability Office (GAO). (2017). *Students need more information to help reduce challenges to transfer college credits.* Author.

Johnson, S. L., & Rush, S. C. (1995). *Reinventing the university: Managing and financing institutions of higher education.* Wiley.

Johnstone, D. B. (2013). Higher educational autonomy and the apportionment of authority among state governments, public multi-campus systems, and member colleges and universities. In J. E. Lane & D. B. Johnstone (Eds)., *Higher education systems 3.0: Harnessing systemness, delivering performance* (pp. 75–100). State University of New York Press.

Kirzner, I. (1973). *Competition and entrepreneurship.* University of Chicago Press.

Lane, J. E., & Johnstone, D. B. (Eds.). (2013). *Higher education systems 3.0: Harnessing systemness, delivering performance.* State University of New York Press.

Lane, J. E. (2018). Data analytics, systemness and predicting student success in college: Examining how the data revolution matters to higher education policy makers. In J. Gagliardi, A. Parnell, & J. Carpenter-Hubin (Eds.), *The analytics revolution in higher education: Big data, organizational learning, and student success.* Stylus.

Lane, J. E. (2019). The drivers of system-level change in higher education. A presentation at the NASH Leadership Academy. Washington, DC, January 2019.

Lee, E. C., & Bowen, F. M. (1971). *The multicampus university: A study of academic governance.* McGraw-Hill.

Lumina Foundation. (n.d.). Goal 2025. https://www.luminafoundation.org/goal_2025

Lumina Foundation. (2019). *A stronger nation: Learning beyond high school builds American talent.* http://strongernation.luminafoundation.org/report/2019/#nation

Ma, D., & Hartley, J. (2017). *Utah's post-secondary participation and completion patterns.* Issue Brief (2017-2). https://ushe.edu/wp-content/uploads/2017/07/2017-2-Five-Year-Participation-and-Completion-David-Ma.pdf

Mayhew, M. J., Rockenbach, A. N., Bowman, N. A., Seifert, T. A., Wolniak, G. C., Pascarella, E. T., & Terenzini, P. T. (2016). *How college affects students* (vol. 3). Jossey-Bass.

McGuiness, A. C., Jr. (2013). The history and evolution of higher education systems in the United States. In J. E. Lane & D. B. Johnstone (Eds.), *Higher education systems 3.0: Harnessing systemness, delivering performance* (pp. 45–74). State University of New York Press.

McLendon, M. K. (2003). State governance reform of higher education: Patterns, trends, and theories of the public policy process.

In J. Smart (Ed.), *Higher education: Handbook of theory and research* (vol. 18, pp. 57–144). Kluwer.

Millard, R. M. (1979). Postsecondary education and "the best interest of the people of the States." *Journal of Higher Education, 50*(2): 24–27.

Organisation for Economic Co-operation and Development (OECD). (2019). *Education at a Glance 2019.* OECD Indicators. OECD.

Pascarella, E., & Terenzini, P. (2005). *How college affects students: A third decade of research* (vol. 2). Jossey-Bass.

Pfeffer, J., & Salancik, G. R. (1978). *The external control of organizations: A resource dependence perspective.* Harper & Row.

Shapiro, D., Dundar, A., Huie, F., Wakhungu, P. K., Bhimdiwali, A., Nathan, A., & Youngsik, H. (2018, July). *Transfer and mobility: A national view of student movement in postsecondary institutions, fall 2011 cohort.* Signature Report No. 15. National Student Clearinghouse Research Center.

Soares, L., Gagliardi, J. S., & Nellum, C. (2017). *The post-traditional learner manifesto revisited.* American Council on Education.

State University of New York (SUNY). (n.d.). SUNY completes. https://www.suny.edu/completion/. Retrieved September 4, 2021.

Thelin, J. R. (2019). *A history of American higher education* (3rd ed.). Johns Hopkins University Press.

Virginia's Community Colleges. (n.d.). *Complete 2021: A six-year strategic plan for Virginia's community colleges.* https://www.vccs.edu/wp-content/uploads/2019/05/Complete-2021-Strategic-Plan-for-Inclusion-in-Grant-Proposals-10-19-2015.pdf. Retrieved September 4, 2021.

Yin, R. K. (2005). *Case study research: Design and methods.* (3rd ed.). Sage.

2

SCALING UP AND SCALING OUT

A Framework for System-Facilitated Innovation in Higher Education

JONATHAN S. GAGLIARDI

ABSTRACT

Higher education reforms that promote student success, close equity gaps, and boost attainment are needed, and systems are seen as a tool to help facilitate and accelerate them. This chapter explores the forces that govern and influence systems, and unpacks the key phases of piloting and scaling innovations, two key components of harnessing systems effectively.

A fundamental question facing higher education systems is whether they are ready and able to evolve in ways that meet the needs of modern students. In order to successfully pilot, incentivize, and scale out innovations that promote student success across multiple campuses, higher education systems must take a contextualized approach. Such an approach, colloquially described by some as "pushing with a feather," represents a departure from the stereotypical mandate-driven, top-down manner that many higher education systems have become known for among their campuses. And even though system-led efforts at transformational change have taken on a decidedly different, more collaborative tone in recent years, the perception that campuses have of their systems has been slow to catch up to reality. To complete their transformation and shed their reputations as state bureaucracies, higher education systems must continue to practice this type of leadership.

Many factors shape how dynamic a higher education system can be, and lofty aspirations and strong implementation plans can be helped or hindered by a number of forces. Some of these forces are more controllable than others. For example, the higher education system office, in collaboration with its campuses, can fashion an internal environment (e.g., structures, incentives, policies) that creates more favorable conditions for student success. Other forces—such as a rogue trustee, an unexpected election outcome, or a sudden economic downturn that results in a negative midterm budget adjustment—are often unpredictable, uncontrollable, and disruptive. Knowledge of those forces and an understanding of the key phases of innovation are vital to system-led change efforts. With that, this chapter examines the internal and external forces that influence system behavior and performance, and provides an innovation framework intended to help guide system-level efforts at transformational change.

TRADITIONAL FUNCTIONS

The relationship between higher education and the state is shaped by the tension between the demands of institutional autonomy and public accountability (Johnstone, 2013; McLendon, 2003), and this balancing act affects how systems evolve and innovate at an elemental level. Public higher education and the needs of the state would be unlinked with too much autonomy. Too much accountability would hamper the ability of a public higher education system to operate effectively (Berdahl, 1971; McGuiness, 2013; McLendon, 2003). This tension is present in all higher education systems, regardless of structure, and is an outgrowth of their primary roles as intermediaries between governments and institutions, and as regulators, allocators, and coordinators (Johnstone, 2013; Lane, 2013).

To strike the right balance between autonomy and accountability, state governments devolve authority and oversight of individual campuses to higher education systems, and these responsibilities typically include the ability to determine institutional mission, academic program review and approval, establishing enrollment management and tuition policies, approval of budgets and dispersal of funds, and the authority to hire campus executives. In turn, the system usually delegates some of its authority to its campuses, which also share authority among various academic and administrative constituents (Johnstone, 2013; McGuiness, 2013). The wide distribution of authority across semi-autonomous and loosely coupled organizations helps preserve stability but can also make it difficult to effect change in a rapid and sustainable manner when evolution is needed (Weick, 1976). This limitation is particularly apparent given the current social, political, and economic climate, which has exposed needed reforms to American higher education, such as increasing student completion, achieving more equitable outcomes, and creating more stable financial models. Because of their unique nature of having governing authority over multiple institutions and being somewhat removed from those institutions, higher education system leaders have a particular opportunity to work to dismantle ineffective structures, creating enabling environments and quickening change. In order to leverage the opportunities provided in such systems effectively, their complexities must first be understood.

UNDERSTANDING SYSTEMS

While useful, previous efforts to categorize systems have offered limited utility due to their static nature and narrow scope. Such typologies tend to map out the universe of systems in a time-specific manner. They also focus on the roles and responsibilities of the system and each campus, in addition to the dispersal of authority and the interplay between them. This leads many to think of systems in a binary fashion: an organization either is or is not a system.

In reality systems have the potential to be nimbler and more diverse than their portrayal in previous research might suggest. A host of factors can influence their operation and performance (e.g., social, political, economic, and technological context). The primary vectors include campus composition (e.g., segmented versus comprehensive) and campus distinctiveness (e.g., consolidated versus multicampus). Secondary dimensions, which can fluctuate over time and vary in definition and execution by state, include (but are not exclusive to) the powers the state has devolved to the governing board, the powers the governing board has devolved to each institution, and board composition, terms, and representation (e.g., gubernatorial appointment, legislature appointed). Statewide election cycles, and other demographic (e.g., shifting populations from rural areas to urban centers), economic (e.g., changing employment opportunities and shifting industries), political (e.g., agendas set by the governor), and technological (e.g., evolution of software to track transfer and mobility) conditions are among the tertiary dimensions that influence, and the influence of each can fluctuate greatly over time.

A variety of often uncontrollable factors influence how agile public higher education systems can be. Still, recent changes, most notably those related to the tertiary forces that shape the desire of the state to enact higher education reforms, necessitate real structural changes in public higher education. Due to the nature of these forces, redesigning public higher education systems is an incremental, nonlinear, and time-intensive process that is prone to fits and starts, and regression without collaboration and a complementary focus on implementation.

Regardless of the inherent difficulty of transformational change, public higher education systems are being tasked with being more dynamic. This will require a fundamental reconsideration of the tools (e.g., policies, structures, incentives) used and the approaches taken by public higher education systems (see chapter 9). Luckily, these new models have begun to emerge, and a new era of systems has begun.

THE IMPETUS FOR A NEW ERA OF SYSTEM-LED INNOVATIONS

Fifty years ago, the expansion of access to postsecondary education led to a period of social innovation within public US colleges and universities. While efforts to increase access were largely successful in terms of diversifying the student body, they fell short of ensuring fully equitable access and, most crucially, outcomes for all students. Today, it appears that higher education is on the verge of evolving again, focusing on improving student outcomes and closing equity gaps. This development is timely as external pressures related to student success and costs, as well as institutional accountability, budgets, and finances, continue to rise. Still, much more will need to be done if systems and the campuses are to change in ways that reflect the needs of the modern student. In reality, the American higher education ecosystem still appears much as it did during a period of unprecedented growth in the 1960s (Berdahl, 1971; Carayannis & Campbell, 2014; Lee & Bowen, 1971; Lyall, 2013). Due to this, the ability of the higher education sector to transform has been cast in doubt.

Systems have encountered difficulties in moving beyond their traditional roles, including coordinating campuses, allocating resources, and developing policies, while also exploring ways to provide centralized services and efficiencies (Gerth, 2010; Martinez & Smith, 2013). This challenge can be explained, in part, by dynamics between systems and campuses that make change more complicated. Context matters, and in some ways the divergent histories, functions, and arrangements of systems and campuses can complicate efforts to evolve (Lane, 2013; McGuiness, 1991). This has resulted in lagging student outcomes, which is especially problematic at a time when upward mobility and economic prosperity are tethered so tightly to postsecondary attainment.

As such, college completion is a social problem that systems are uniquely poised to solve if harnessed effectively. They are doing so by embracing new roles and partnerships to navigate beyond barriers to success. Some of these new roles for systems include (a) providing shared services, (b) setting data-informed systemwide goals and targets for student success, (c) offering solutions that can be customized for institutions based on their traits, (d) leveraging the power of the convening, and (e) using their platform to incentivize and scale out evidence-based innovations (Gagliardi et al., 2015; King, 2013; Lane, 2013; Lane & Johnstone, 2013; Lyall, 2013).

INNOVATION AND SOCIAL INNOVATION

While innovation is an ambiguous phenomenon, definitions of it include introducing something new or different, making changes, and adding value (O'Sullivan & Dooley, 2009; Quinn, 1985). Innovation is complex; it requires the integration of a diverse set of variables and processes and can occur instantaneously or incrementally, as well as intentionally or organically (Kanter, 1985/2000; Martinez & Smith, 2013; O'Sullivan & Dooley, 2009). It involves creativity, purpose, and mindful and deliberate design, which are contextualized in ways that enhance organizations and people (Drucker, 1988; Rosenfeld & Servo, 1991). Diffusion and adoption are signs that an innovation has been successful, as it has created a new standard for doing things (Schumpeter, 1934/2000). Innovation is also cyclical and reaches its fullest potential when advanced in a continuous fashion. If innovation is not approached in this manner, it can become stagnant, which can lead to negative consequences that eclipse the value that the innovation was designed to create. Eventually, these unintended consequences can be perpetuated, which eventually begets the need for additional, more difficult, and dramatic change (Rogers, 2003).

The study of innovation and perpetuation is one of contrasts, despite their cyclical and related natures. Each requires different organizational arrangements and leadership styles. Innovation requires cultivation, whereas perpetuation benefits from conservation (Hanan, 1976; Kanter, 1985/2000; Stevenson & Gumpert, 1985). The source of innovation is often unpredictable, and defining success can be a painstaking and inaccurate process, making it hard to know how to monitor and track progress. The development process can be costly, and the returns take a long time to materialize (Biggadike, 1979; Quinn, 1979, 1985). Innovations can produce large volumes of knowledge that are difficult to chronicle and diffuse effectively, which can prevent the full potential of an innovation from being realized and lead to stagnation. Stalled innovations may also result in deeply entrenched structures, cultures, and arrangements, making change efforts increasingly difficult and complex. Innovations that anticipate and overcome these challenges, however, often benefit from an environment that is flexible and interconnected. They also have committed leadership and diverse revenue streams. Successful innovations are often designed as a solution to a specific social challenge (Kanter, 1985/2000), as is evidenced by the increasing popularity of social innovation, which emphasizes solutions to shared problems and positive social impact (Fifka & Idowu, 2013; Phills et al., 2008).

IMPORTANCE OF ADOPTION AND SCALING TO SUCCESSFUL SOCIAL INNOVATIONS

Osburg and Schmidpeter (2013) suggest that innovations of all kinds require time and maturation. Their lifecycle model includes various stages that rely on different skills, infrastructure, and resources. Santos and colleagues (2013) point to the identification of a problem and the development of a solution as a critical first step. Through a process of trial and error and refinement and revision, sustainable and replicable models can be created. Subsequently, the development of a business model is of priority, as is growth management. Once proof-of-concept has been achieved, it can be diffused to various stakeholders and actors who can contribute to systematizing change (Mulgan, 2007; Santos et al., 2013). Models that describe this process vary in the number of stages and evolution points that they include, but each model focuses on the cycle of creating the solution rather than the cycle of implementing the solution (Baron & Shane, 2005; Kuratko & Hodgetts, 2003; Osburg & Schmidpeter, 2013; Sahlman et al., 1999; Santos et al., 2013; Timmons & Spinelli, 2004).

For social innovations specifically, which are those often undertaken within higher education, developing a solution with a complementary implementation plan helps to maximize the impact they have on society (Osburg & Schmidpeter, 2013; Santos et al., 2013). There are five lifecycle stages to social innovations: idea creation, experimentation, organization, systematizing and scaling, and sustainability (Elkington et al., 2010; Mulgan, 2010). See table 2.1 for a list and description of the key elements of social innovations, in addition to questions for consideration during their design.

Table 2.1. Phases of Innovation

Phase	Description	Key Questions
Ideation	• The point of ideation that comes from identifying a problem and finding a solution; the moment of opportunity recognition.	• What is/are the problem(s)? • What is/are the solution(s)? • How do they connect? • Who do they impact? • What are the externalities?
Experimentation	• The process of hypothesizing, information gathering, and initial experimentation. This could be considered a beta-test phase.	• Is there evidence of impact? • How did early adoption efforts succeed? Why? • Where did they fall short? Why? • Who are the experts at implementing this?
Organizing	• Reinventing and refining based on learnings from previous experiments. At this stage, a proof-of-concept is ready to be used to generate stakeholder buy-in and investment.	• Who will be part of the initial cohort? • Is there evidence of commitment and passion? • What investments will be or have stakeholders made? • Within and across systems, who are peers? Who have the same contexts (traits, demands, characteristics, and strengths)? How do you connect them?
Systematizing and scaling	• Developing an ecosystem of change agents who advocate the enactment of your innovation. Cultivating a critical mass who begins to change what is considered to be the norm. Developing networks, cataloging how end users have tailored the innovation to suit their context.	• Of the first cohort, where are the bright spots? • Who did this well? • How would they describe success? • Will they serve as teachers and diffusers of the lessons learned? • What tools were developed? • What obstacles arose?
Sustainability and new innovation	• Reaching the point of scale and adoption, where the innovation has now become the standard and complementary cycles of innovation begin anew.	• How do you ensure adoption? • What will make this sustainable? • How will this be communicated, diffused, and replicated? • Who will be a part of the second cohort? • How can you continue to innovate through refinement and revision of this process?

Note: Adapted from Mulgan (2007).

IMPORTANCE OF INNOVATION FAILURES AND STAKEHOLDER-CENTERED DESIGN

The problems that leaders are attempting to solve in higher education are complex, as every problem continues to evolve in real time; solutions can have unintended consequences, and we are often having a direct impact on the lives of students, faculty, and staff. So, it is important to look at what we already know about innovation failures, so we can try to best situate our efforts for success. But failure is an inevitable part of the overall innovation picture; no matter how good the ideas, some simply do not work for any number of reasons.

What the literature tells us is that innovation failures often occur when design elements are not end-user focused, communication is sparse and not tailored, stakeholders are not engaged throughout the process, continuous improvement is not pursued, and successful organizational routines are abandoned rather than simultaneously strengthened (Rogers, 2003). Further, social innovations often fall short of expectations for various reasons, including cost; not being effective enough; externalities, or costs or benefits that affect a population that did not choose to incur said cost or benefit; and inaction by people or organizations in a position to create change, which can occur due to both a lack of incentives to act and an insufficient voice to be heard.

Despite negative connotations associated with failure, many successful innovations begin from a previous failure (Seelos & Mair, 2012). It is important to recognize that the real value of innovation comes incrementally and through continuous learning; there is no silver bullet. By learning from failures, successful innovation becomes more likely. Learning from failures involves stakeholder engagement and communication, which should be primary drivers of the design process (Bhattacharya, 2013; Crabtree, 2012). Engaging multiple stakeholders throughout each of the phases of an innovation creates ownership and buy-in, as well as insight, if done properly. "In sum, if one follows a stakeholder-centric approach, there are four steps to successfully generating social innovation ideas: articulating unmet social needs, generating ideas to meet those needs, distilling ideas, and selecting ideas to pursue" (Bhattacharya, 2013, p. 149). This approach hinges on effective and customized communication, which can help combat entrenched attitudes, behaviors, and cultures. It can be enhanced through evidence and a data-informed approach, which together create a wealth of information to drive continuous improvement and effective collaboration.

In reality, innovations rarely live up to the early hype and inflated expectations generated by initial success (Edmonson, 2011; Gartner, 2019). Similarly, the shortcomings of innovations that are deemed failures are often overblown. Valuable opportunities for organization-specific learning and reflection are lost because of the powerful and negative stigma of failure. Edmonson's (2011) spectrum of reasons for failure highlight that some failures are blameworthy, others are praiseworthy, and many fall somewhere in the middle. Failure is unavoidable in complex systems, like colleges and universities, and the introduction of new ideas and processes are bound to lead to system failures, which are evident in a number of the case studies that follow.

The University of Texas System's Total Educational Experience (TEx) was launched in 2014 by the Institute for Transformational Learning (ITL), which itself was developed in 2012 as a startup-like technology initiative. At the time of its creation, TEx was an unprecedented effort by a public higher education system to develop and scale out a personalized, competency-based education. The ITL (and TEx) closed in 2018, largely due to the inability to generate self-sustaining revenue streams and create a viable business plan. Despite this, the initiative did positively impact the development and organization of online programs and materials (Satija & Najmabadi, 2018). Moreover, the approach taken to concepts of personalized pathways, interactive courseware, micro credentials, bilingual content, and simulations have the potential to have a lasting impact on higher education (Lederman, 2018).

Innovations also depend on leadership, culture, and continuity, and a disruption in any of these three dimensions can lead to setbacks or stagnation. In the case of Degree Compass, a predictive analytics tool developed at Austin Peay State University and later scaled across the Tennessee Board of Regents (TBR), initial gains in retention and graduation rates sparked a great deal of interest. However, since then, they have leveled off. Tristan Denley, who primarily oversaw the development of the tool, left Austin Peay for the TBR, which as part of the 2016 Focus Act lost its six universities (Sher, 2018). Denley eventually left for the University System of Georgia. Without a system or champions, Degree Compass was slowly deprioritized over time. In this case, the loss of the systems governing authority and leadership transitions have had an impact on the perceived effectiveness of the tool (Johnson, 2018).

Systems can incentivize cross-campus collaboration and the design of experiments and prototypes. They have a unique capacity to identify common opportunities and challenges among campuses, and have the wherewithal to provide resources and supports for small-scale prototypes of promise. They are also positioned to house innovations independently of individual campuses and ensure that they are responsibly scaled and sustained. Where innovations fall short of expectations, systems can also ensure that all is done to learn from them.

THE CONSEQUENCES OF INNOVATION

How well one manages to engage, communicate, and codevelop an innovation with stakeholders has implications for its effects. The consequences of an innovation can be categorized in three ways: desirable versus undesirable, direct versus indirect, and anticipated versus unanticipated (Rogers, 2003). Depending on the nature of the consequences, further reinventions will be required, hence the importance of continuous improvement. According to Rogers (2003), if special attention is not paid to stakeholder-centered design, socioeconomic gaps widen because groups perched atop socioeconomic hierarchies are more likely to be early adopters. These groups enjoy information of higher quality and volume, stronger networks, and greater resources (Rogers, 2003). To the extent possible, successful social innovations attempt to accommodate this reality. Table 2.2 offers a review of some of the critical elements of successful social innovations. In many ways, expanding access to higher education is a case study of the intended and unintended consequences of social innovations.

Table 2.2. Critical Elements of Successful Social Innovations

What?	Key Questions
Understand the value added and life cycle of innovation	• What is the value added society? • What makes this process or product novel? • How long will it take to see return on investment? • Will this occur after the implementation life cycle?
Establishing central control and transitioning to autonomy	• How do you start with central control? • What elements are nonnegotiable? • How do you transition to greater autonomy? • What flexibility will be needed, and when?
Progressively and continuously forming coalitions	• What relationships need to be formulated? • What is the correct volume of participants? • When do these need to be developed? • Who will aid in their development?
Developing new devices and solutions to embed change	• Do new roles need to be created? • Are there new rules, policies, and devices that are necessary?
Dissolving boundaries and brokering a dialogue between stakeholders	• How do these stakeholders interact? • How can other efforts and stakeholders amplify this? • What are our individual and shared responsibilities?
Cultivating evolutionary and revolutionary leadership	• Is there sufficient follow-through at leadership levels across the initiative? • How will leadership gather and connect people? • Can leadership see connections, envision new ideas, and chart a future course?
Reinventing innovations in customized and improved ways	• How can you help organizations adopt innovations in customized ways? • What systems do you have in place to monitor and track progress as it occurs? • Are you communicating reinventions contextually to adopters?
Understanding the consequences	• What are the possible: Desirable and undesirable consequences? Direct and indirect consequences? Anticipated and unanticipated consequences? • How are you planning to mitigate negative consequences? • What social innovations will be needed to overcome new problems?

Note: Adapted from Rogers (2003) and Santos et al. (2013).

SOCIAL INNOVATION IN HIGHER EDUCATION:
EXPANDING ACCESS BY IMPROVING STUDENT OUTCOMES

One of the preeminent social problems faced by the United States in the 1940s was a need for a more highly educated citizenry. There were concerns that returning soldiers would struggle with their transition to civilian life, from both social and economic perspectives. Uncertainty surrounding national security was on the rise due in part to advances in weaponry. A looming Cold War magnified international tensions and competition, particularly with the USSR. At that time, our collective consciousness was drifting toward the Space Race. However, the most important race was not occurring outside of our atmosphere; it was happening in our classrooms and our lecture halls. Facing serious deficits in educational attainment, Bush (1945) wrote: "Higher education in this country is largely for those who have the means. . . . There are talented individuals in every segment of the population, but with few exceptions those without the means of buying higher education go without it. Here is a tremendous waste of the greatest resource of a nation—the intelligence of its citizens" (p. 25).

The President's Commission on Higher Education (1947) further highlighted the need for social mobility and economic growth by elaborating on challenges that included access barriers, economic barriers, restricted curriculum, and racial and religious barriers. At the same time during which this social problem was emerging, a series of policy and organizational innovations were designed to solve it. Policies such as the Servicemen's Readjustment Act of 1944 (commonly known as the GI Bill) and the Higher Education Act of 1965 were created to promote a shift in higher education access from the elite to the masses. Further, a series of organizational innovations occurred with the same goals in mind (Brint & Karabel, 1989; Lee & Bowen, 1971).[1] This included the development[2] of community colleges;[3] an increase in the number of public universities; and the continued evolution of higher education systems, coordinating boards, and multicampus universities (Brint & Karabel, 1989; Lee & Bowen, 1971; McGuiness, 2013). These policies and structures, each aimed at expanding access and opportunity, were social innovations and helped frame higher education as a public good. While the mass expansion of higher education has been a successful social innovation, unintended consequences have emerged, particularly as enrollment demographics have changed and outcomes have been increasingly prioritized.

UNFORESEEN CONSEQUENCES OF PREVIOUS INNOVATIONS

Emphasizing Access and Working against Completion

As the number of campuses increased to meet the demands for increased access to postsecondary education, a complex web of horizontal and vertical structures was also put into place. These developments led to a loosely coupled system of higher education, and the missions and purposes of its constituent—separate but newly connected—organizations were vague (Cohen & March, 1986; Lee & Bowen, 1971). According to Keeling and colleagues (2007), this approach was used to "allow for creative thinking, and to respect—and even encourage—the autonomy of different disciplines" (p. 1), which even then was not easily aligned with growing demands for assessment and accountability. Within this decentralized campus structure is a mixture of cultures across disciplinary and administrative units that have differing interests and goals. These differences can be barriers to broader institutional objectives focused on improving student outcomes (Clark, 1963/2000; Keeling et al., 2007; Schroeder, 1999).

The parallel evolution of systems and coordinating boards across states, with some states such as New York and Texas creating multiple systems, added even greater complexity to the higher education landscape. These governance structures were designed to employ organizational techniques that were adopted from industry and government to centralize authority, consequently shifting some control away from campuses. Lee and Bowen (1971) allude to a "largely hidden battle . . . over how much less campus authority there would be" (p. xii). As a result, natural tensions emerged between campuses and governance structures. Decentralized campuses and disciplines that were both academic and autonomous—and which had developed over decades, if not longer—now were grappling with centralized and administrative governance structures (Lane, 2013). While these tensions have always been present, their unintended consequences have become more apparent as time has passed, and students and the demands placed on higher education have changed. These horizontal misalignments make an approach based on *systemness* difficult to realize, despite its apparent benefits (Zimpher, 2013). They can lead to inefficiencies and redundancies that are artifacts of less connected social and higher education structures.

A Culture Focused on Perpetuation Rather than Innovation

In the post–World War II era, a culture was created that prioritized ideation and standardization rather than innovation, which includes adoption, reinvention, customization, and sustainability. These policy and organizational innovations developed their own structures, functions, and fields, each of which had its own set of producers, consumers, and agencies, ultimately shaping higher education into what is today (DiMaggio & Powell, 1983). These processes serve as forms of oversight, by which actors in a given field are indoctrinated. Structures serve to provide stability, but they are not changed easily, and efforts to undo them are difficult by design.

Higher education is no stranger to this phenomenon. In addition to the internal tensions and resistance that arise between campuses and governance structures, tensions exist within campuses and among faculty members. The nature of faculty training and status leads many instructors to "cherish autonomy from direct control by administrative authorities" (Hearn, 2006, p. 5). Demands for research productivity have led to a separation between teaching and research (Brint, 2011; Rhoades, 2012). Reward systems encourage senior or tenure-track faculty to conduct research rather than focus on teaching (Rhoades, 2007, 2012). These incentives are sometimes in tension with a focus on student success at the undergraduate level (Ehrenberg & Zhang, 2004).

In addition to the complex web of tensions that exist within campuses and between disciplines, as well as across campuses and their governance structures, external pressures also stem from the role of governance structures as boundary spanners. Over the last decade, stakeholders have developed alternative perceptions about the purpose, value, and function of higher education. This shift has created great turmoil, as traditional ways of doing things are coming under intense scrutiny at the hand of new agendas, purposes, and goals (Fligstein & McAdam, 2012; Scott, 2005, 2015). This change has disrupted the social, political, and economic capital around which higher education has traditionally been organized (Bourdieu, 1986). As conditions continue to change rapidly, the benefits of previous social innovations will diminish while the effects of unintended consequences will be magnified (Rogers, 2003).

REALIGNING HIGHER EDUCATION TOWARD COMPLETION THROUGH SYSTEMS

Higher education systems are useful tools for encouraging colleges and universities to realign from a focus on student access to a focus on student completion—a daunting challenge that has not been solved despite enormous political and financial investments. By, setting systemwide priorities, driving innovation, providing shared services and coordinating alternative pathways that include online learning, systems and campuses are leveraging one another in unprecedented ways (Mintz, 2014). The current emphasis on degrees has redistributed the responsibility of social mobility and economic growth more equally among research universities, comprehensive institutions, and community colleges. Due to their ability to serve as laboratories for innovation, hubs for analysis, and gatherers of organizational and environmental intelligence, systems are able to create economies of scale that are essential to meeting that shared responsibility, as well as current and future demands. Systems are increasingly important, and identifying examples of system-led innovations is critical to ensuring social mobility and economic growth. The following examples illustrate the vital role that systems play in innovating and scaling.

Theme: Focusing on Collective Impact for Successful Innovation

As evidenced in the case studies in this volume, systems are increasingly convening stakeholders from across institutions to tackle common challenges. Some of these groups may be based on similar roles (e.g., provosts, enrollment managers, or advisors) or based on a particular issue to be addressed (e.g., implementing a new transfer policy). This approach leads to a more comprehensive inventory of problems and potential solutions, in addition to the risks and rewards associated with each.

By generating consensus around opportunities and challenges, and identifying potential solutions with a sound body of evidence, system leaders can promote the effective organization of campuses that see value in adopting such innovations as well as use their capacity and central positioning to gather evidence and monitor progress in addition to serving as a hub for organizational intelligence.

In large systems, one strategy may be to focus on organizing a group of like-minded campuses that are ready to adopt an evidence-based approach, as it can leverage coordinated efforts that can be quickly disbursed and diffused by working with coalitions of the willing. This strategy also negates the potential backlash that is possible if campuses perceive system action as an attempt to exert authority rather than as a resource. This progressive and continuous formation allows implementation to be devolved to the campuses that are willing to adopt the solution, without being too prescriptive.

In the cases in this volume, systems developed networks among the adopting campuses, acting as a platform for coordination and information exchange, which helped to lower walls between distinct campuses. Systems that guided the organic development of communities surrounding specific innovations prompted greater collaboration and fostered dialogue between campuses. In some cases, to overcome barriers to sustainability, systems also worked to generate philanthropic and/or government funding to support the interventions for the longer term.

CONCLUSIONS AND IMPLICATIONS

The preceding discussion used the lenses of innovation and social innovation to explore how US higher education institutions are innovating to shift from a student access agenda to a student completion agenda. As part of this chapter, a number of ongoing efforts to improve student outcomes were reviewed. This section identifies five transitions that may be needed to further advance this work and that may have implications for leaders of systems as they attempt to improve student outcomes and close equity gaps.

Transition 1: Rather than Perpetuate, Innovate

In direct response to growing national concerns, US higher education reform efforts after World War II focused on expanding access and included the creation of policies and organizations that supported that effort. As such, they represented a social innovation, in that by expanding access to higher education, they promoted social mobility and economic growth for the entire country. Data suggest that policies and practices that promoted access to colleges and universities were largely successful in that they did increase access to postsecondary education; however, because of the continual expansion in terms of students coming into higher education, there was less concern about the need to support students toward completion. Now, these innovations require reinvention to accommodate the shift in emphasis toward student completion. As previously mentioned, reinvention and continuous innovation are difficult to achieve, particularly when they involve such a varied landscape of organizations and policies, each with their own cultures and arrangements and data that have over time shifted from innovating to perpetuating.

Transition 2: Move from Isolated to Integrated

By the time the need to shift from access to completion was identified as a social problem, the structures, arrangements, rewards, and behaviors of the myriad horizontal and vertical structures in higher education were entrenched. This situation led to isolated fields and organizations that were naturally in tension with one another. For decades, systems, campuses, and divisions acted in isolation, toward different ends, making it difficult for the goal of completion to take hold across systems and campuses. The function of time and entrenchment made such a shift more difficult for a variety of reasons. One of the unintended consequences of this culture of isolation was the widening of equity gaps, which has become more pronounced as the need for more interconnected campuses has risen due to changes in student demographics and enrollment patterns.

Transition 3: Aggregation to Disaggregation

Broadening access and ongoing population changes—coupled with an increasing student cost burden, advances and technology, and more transient and diverse students—rapidly multiplied the contexts and challenges faced by incoming students. The development of equally disaggregated data and intervention strategies did not match the pace of change, however. Thus, one-size-fits-all solutions did not meet the needs of students, contributing to a widening of equity gaps despite wholesale increases in access and completions over the last half century.

Transition 4: A Retrospective Approach to a Prospective One

Fundamental misalignments are reflected in how we monitor and track progress. Our current data infrastructure reflects a homogeneous student population that has disappeared slowly over the last few decades. Such is evidenced by mandated compliance reports, including what is required for submission to the Integrated Postsecondary Education Data System (IPEDS), which still focuses on six-year graduation rates at one institution, and which fails to disaggregate student populations in ways that include low-income and underrepresented minority students. This problem is further reflected in the roles and functions of decision analytics and institutional research functions at systems, which remain topically stove-piped and still focus on transactional reports versus the strategic use of data. These functions are increasingly relied upon to respond to a sea of demands and compliance reports, while also conducting deeper predictive analytics. Despite this growing role, they lack the support and infrastructure needed to balance yesterday's compliance reports with matters more closely aligned with present and future demands on higher education, such as dramatic increases in completion. While these functions have attempted to migrate from explanatory to exploratory analyses that are more cross-functional, realistically they still have yet to jump from looking more closely into the past to peering into the future. There are a few examples of successful transitions, such as the examples previously discussed in this chapter, but there is still a long way to go if more customized, student-focused solutions are to be offered effectively with an eye toward completion and organizational effectiveness.

System leaders can strengthen their efforts at innovation by understanding the primary, secondary, and tertiary factors that can influence them. Doing so requires a unified vision and evidence-based approach to leveraging their position as boundary spanners and the distinctive assets of their campuses to promote student success. By further customizing and continuously improving these efforts, system leaders can create advantageous partnerships among the campuses they serve. Shifting the way data are used from a transactional model toward one that is more strategic can help system leaders allocate resources to the issues that matter most. Changing the approach to student success from one that is aggregated to disaggregated can help in creating programs and services that are designed with the varied challenges of diverse students in mind. System leaders can empower and support cohorts of campuses that are ready and willing to be more integrated by offering tools, data, incentives, and expert and technical assistance, where possible. Additionally, system leaders can help create meaningful change by focusing on the key phases of innovation, which go beyond opportunity recognition, and which entail experimentation, organization, scaling, and sustainability. By doing so, they can avoid stagnation that over time can make improvement a daunting task. The cases presented here represent efforts undertaken by systems to do just that, and the subsequent conclusions and transitions observed are a means to bridge theory and practice and are designed to help guide system leaders as they innovate in ways that promote equitable access and outcomes.

CHAPTER 2 TAKEAWAYS

- Historic and bureaucratic barriers cause systems to perpetuate status quo.

- The scale and authority of a system also present opportunities for facilitating large-scale change.

- The increased focus of state officials on completion and equity gaps may be a key driver for moving systems to become problem solvers.

- The key is to balance institutional distinctiveness with the benefits of greater collaboration.

NOTES

1. The Carnegie Commission (1967–1973) offered suggestions for a hierarchical system of higher education that pursued both quality and equality (Brint & Karabel, 1989, p. 104).
2. According to Lee and Bowen (1971), between 1958–1959 and 1968–1969, the number of governing and coordinating boards grew from 164 to 198 (+34). In that same time frame, the number of systems grew from 63 to 84 (+21). In total, the number of public universities, four-year colleges, and two-year colleges was 855 in 1968.
3. Within 30 years of the community college boom, these schools would constitute over 40 percent of all undergraduate enrollments and over half of all entering students (Brint & Karabel, 1989, p. 103).

REFERENCES

Baron, R. A., & Shane, S. (2005). *Entrepreneurship: A process perspective*. Thomson/South-Western.

Bhattacharya, C. B. (2013). The importance of marketing for social innovation. In T. Osburg & R. Schmidpeter (Eds.), *Social innovation: Solutions for a sustainable future* (pp. 147–154). Springer.

Biggadike, R. (1979). The risky business of diversification. *Harvard Business Review, 57*(3), 103–111.

Bourdieu, P. (1986). The forms of capital. In J. G. Richardson (Ed.), *Handbook of theory and research for the sociology of education* (pp. 242–258). Greenwood Press.

Berdahl, R. O. (1971). *Statewide coordination of higher education.* American Council on Education.

Brint, S. S. (2011). Focus on the classroom: Movements to reform college teaching, 1980–2008. In J. C. Hermanowicz (Ed.), *The American academic profession: Transformation in contemporary higher education* (pp. 44–91). Johns Hopkins University Press.

Brint, S. S., & Karabel, J. (1989). *The diverted dream: Community colleges and the promise of educational opportunity in America, 1900–1985.* Oxford University Press.

Bush, V. (1945). *Science, the endless frontier: A report to the president.* U.S. Government Printing Office.

Carayannis, E. G., & Campbell, D. F. J. (2014). Developed democracies versus emerging autocracies: Arts, democracy, and innovation in Quadruple Helix innovation systems. *Journal of Innovation and Entrepreneurship, 3*(12). doi:10.1186/s13731-014-0012-2

Clark, B. R. 1963/2000. Faculty organization and authority. In M. C. Brown II (Ed.), *Organization and governance in higher education* (5th ed., pp. 119–127). Pearson Custom.

Cohen, M. D., & March, J. G. (1986). *Leadership and ambiguity: The American college president.* Harvard Business School Press.

Crabtree, J. (2012, September 12). Visionary tactics. *Financial Times.* http://www.ft.com/intl/cms/s/2/7d3afcde-fb0b-11e1-87ae-00144feabdc0.html#axzz3TX8fzv12

DiMaggio, P. J., & Powell, W. (1983). The iron cage revisited: Institutional isomorphism and collective rationality in organizational fields. *American Sociological Review, 48*, 147–160. doi:10.2307/2095101

Drucker, P. F. (1988). The coming of the new organization. *Harvard Business Review, 66*(1), 3–11.

Edmondson, A. C. (2011). Strategies for learning from failure. *Harvard Business Review, 89*(4), 48–55.

Ehrenberg, R. L., & Zhang, L. (2004). *Do tenured and non-tenure track faculty matter?* (National Bureau of Economic Research Working Paper No. 10695). http://www.nber.org/papers/w10695.pdf

Elkington, J., Hartigan, P., & Litovsky, A. (2010). From enterprise to ecosystem: Rebooting the scale debate. In P. N. Bloom & E. Skloot (Eds.), *Scaling social impact: New thinking* (pp. 83–102). Palgrave Macmillan.

Fifka, M. S., & Idowu, S. O. (2013). Sustainability and social innovation. In T. Osburg & R. Schmidpeter (Eds.), *Social innovation: Solutions for a sustainable future* (pp. 309–316). Springer.

Fligstein, N., & McAdam, D. (2012). *A theory of fields.* Oxford University Press.

Gagliardi, J. S., Martin, R. R., Wise, K., & Blaich, C. (2015). The system effect: Scaling high-impact practices across campuses. *New Directions for Higher Education*, 15–26. doi:10.1002/he.20119

Gartner. 2019. *Gartner hype cycle.* https://www.gartner.com/en/research/methodologies/gartner-hype-cycle

Gerth, D. R. (2010). *The people's university: A history of the California State University.* Berkeley Public Policy Press.

Hanan, M. (1976). Venturing: Think small to stay strong. *Harvard Business Review, 54*(3), 139–148.

Hearn, J. C. (2006). *Student success: What research suggests for policy and practice.* National Center for Education Statistics. http://nces.ed.gov/npec/pdf/synth_Hearn.pdf

Higher Education Act of 1965. (1965). 1 U.S.C. §§ 101-804.

Johnson, S. (2018). *Are you still there? How a "Netflix" model for advising lost its luster.* https://www.edsurge.com/news/2018-03-15-are-you-still-there-how-a-netflix-model-for-advising-lost-its-luster

Johnstone, D. B. (2013). Higher educational autonomy and the apportionment of authority among state governments, public multi-campus systems, and member colleges and universities. In J. E. Lane & D. B. Johnstone (Eds.), *Higher education systems 3.0: Harnessing systemness, delivering performance* (pp. 75–100). State University of New York Press.

Kanter, R. M. (1985/2000). When a thousand flowers bloom: Structural, collective, and social conditions for innovation in organization. In R. Swedberg (Ed.), *Entrepreneurship: The social science view* (pp. 167–209). Oxford University Press.

Keeling, R. P., Underhile, R., & Wall, A. F. (2007). Horizontal and vertical structures: The dynamics of organization in higher education. *Liberal Education, 93*(4). http://www.aacu.org/publications-research/periodicals/horizontal-and-vertical-structures-dynamics-organization-higher

King, C. J. (2013). Board governance of public university systems: Balancing institutional independence and system coordination. In J. E. Lane & D. B. Johnstone (Eds.), *Higher education systems 3.0: Harnessing systemness, delivering performance* (pp. 149–168). State University of New York Press.

Kuratko, D. F., & Hodgetts, R. M. (2003). *Entrepreneurship: Theory, process, and practice.* Thomson.

Lane, J. E. (2013). Higher education systems 3.0: Adding value to states and institutions. In J. E. Lane & D. B. Johnstone (Eds.), *Higher education systems 3.0: Harnessing systemness, delivering performance* (pp. 1–26). State University of New York Press.

Lane, J. E., & Johnstone, D. B. (Eds.). (2013). *Higher education systems 3.0: Harnessing systemness, delivering performance.* State University of New York Press.

Lederman, D. (2018). *Lessons learned from a $75 million failed experiment.* https://www.insidehighered.com/digital-learning/article/2018/02/21/lessons-learned-shuttering-universitys-internal-digital-learning

Lee, E. C., & Bowen, F. M. (1971). *The multicampus university: A study on academic governance.* McGraw-Hill.

Lyall, C. C. (2013). Reorganizing higher education systems: By drift or design? In J. E. Lane & D. B. Johnstone (Eds.), *Higher education systems 3.0: Harnessing systemness, delivering performance* (pp. 149–168). State University of New York Press.

Martinez, M., & Smith, B. (2013). Systems, ecosystems, and change in state-level public higher education. In J. E. Lane & D. B. Johnstone (Eds.), *Higher education systems 3.0: Harnessing systemness, delivering performance* (pp. 169–192). State University of New York Press.

McGuiness, A. C., Jr. (1991). *Perspective on the current status of and emerging issues for public multicampus higher education systems* (AGB Occasional Paper No. 3). Association of Governing Boards of Colleges and Universities.

McGuiness, A. C., Jr. (2013). The history and evolution of higher education systems in the United States. In J. E. Lane & D. B.

Johnstone (Eds.), *Higher education systems 3.0: Harnessing systemness, delivering performance* (pp. 45–71). State University of New York Press.

McLendon, M. K. (2003). State governance reform of higher education: Patterns, trends, and theories of the public policy process. In J. Smart (Ed.), *Higher education: Handbook of theory and research* (vol. 18, pp. 57–143). Kluwer.

Millet, J. D. (1984). *Conflict in higher education: State government coordination versus institutional independence*. Jossey-Bass.

Mintz, S. (2014, March 26). The shifting role of university systems. *Inside Higher Ed*. https://www.insidehighered.com/blogs/higher-ed-beta/shifting-role-university-systems

Mulgan, G. (2007). *Social innovation: What it is, why it matters and how it can be accelerated*. Young Foundation. http://youngfoundation.org/publications/social-innovation-what-it-is-why-it-matters-how-it-can-be-accelerated/

Mulgan, G. (2010). Measuring social value. *Stanford Social Innovation Review*. http://www.ssireview.org/articles/entry/measuring_social_value

Osburg, T., & Schmidpeter, R. (2013). *Social innovation: Solutions for a sustainable future*. Springer.

O'Sullivan, D., & Dooley, L. (2009). *Applying innovation*. Sage.

Phills, J. A., Jr., Deiglmeier, K., & Miller, D. T. (2008). Rediscovering social innovation. *Stanford Social Innovation Review*. http://www.ssireview.org/articles/entry/rediscovering_social_innovation

President's Commission on Higher Education. (1947). *Establishing the goals: Higher education for American democracy*. Hathi Trust. http://catalog.hathitrust.org/Record/001117586

Quinn, J. B. (1979). Technological innovation, entrepreneurship, and strategy. *Sloan Management Review, 20*(3), 19–30.

Quinn, J. B. (1985). Managing innovation chaos. *Harvard Business Review, 63*(3), 73–84.

Rhoades, G. (2007). Technology-enhanced courses and a mode III organization of instructional work. *Tertiary Education and Management, 13*, 1–17. doi:10.1080/13583880601145496

Rhoades, G. (2012). *Faculty engagement to enhance student attainment*. American Council on Education. http://www.acenet.edu/news-room/Documents/Faculty-Engagement-to-Enhance-Student-Attainment--Rhoades.pdf

Rogers, E. M. (2003). *Diffusion of innovations*. Free Press.

Rosenfeld, R., & Servo, J. C. (1991). Facilitating innovation in large organizations. In J. C. Henry & D. Walker (Eds.), *Managing innovation* (pp. 28–40). Sage.

Santos, F., Salvado, J. C., Lopo de Carvalho, I., & Schulte, U. G. (2013). The life cycle of social innovations. In T. Osburg & R. Schmidpeter (Eds.), *Social innovation: Solutions for a sustainable future* (pp. 183–196). Springer.

Satija, N., & Najmabadi, S. (2018). *"Costly and Unsustainable": After spending $75 million, a troubled UT System technology institute shuts its doors.* https://www.texastribune.org/2018/02/07/ut-system-shuts-down-major-endowment-funded-initiative/

Schroeder, C. C. 1999. Forging educational partnerships that advance student learning. In G. S. Blimling & E. J. Whitt (Eds.), *Good practice in student affairs: Principles to foster student learning* (pp. 133–156). Jossey-Bass.

Schumpeter, J. A. (1934/2000). Entrepreneurship as innovation. In R. Swedberg (Ed.), *Entrepreneurship: The social science view* (pp. 51–75). Oxford University Press.

Scott, W. R. (2005). Institutional theory: Contributing to a theoretical research program. In K. G. Smith & M. A. Hitt (Eds.), *Great minds in management: The process of theory development* (pp. 460–484). Oxford University Press.

Scott, W. R. (2015). Education in America: Multiple field perspectives. In M. W. Kirst & M. L. Stevens, *Remaking college: The changing ecology of higher education* (pp. 19–38). Stanford University Press.

Seelos, C., & Mair, J. (2012). Innovation is not the holy grail. *Stanford Social Innovation Review.* http://www.ssireview.org/articles/entry/innovation_is_not_the_holy_grail

Servicemen's Readjustment Act of 1944. (1944). 1 U.S.C. §§ 1767-24.

Sher, A. (2018). *Tennessee governor's plan to restructure UT board of trustees draws concerns.* https://www.timesfreepress.com/news/politics/state/story/2018/feb/19/hamiltcounty-trustees-ut-board-trustees-could/464036/

Stevenson, H. H., & Gumpert, D. E. (1985). The heart of entrepreneurship. *Harvard Business Review, 85*(2), 85–94.

SUNY Task Force on Remediation. (2012). *The SUNY pathway to success.* State University of New York. http://blog.suny.edu/2013/01/2012-year-in-review-chancellors-task-force-on-remediation/

Timmons, J. A., & Spinelli, S. (2004). *New venture creation: Entrepreneurship for the 21st century*. McGraw-Hill.

Weick, K. E. (1976). Education organizations as loosely coupled systems. *Administrative Science Quarterly, 21*, 105–122. doi:10.2307/2391875

Zimpher, N. L. (2013). Systemness: Unpacking the value of higher education systems. In J. E. Lane & D. B. Johnstone (Eds.), *Higher education systems 3.0: Harnessing systemness, delivering performance* (pp. 27–44). State University of New York Press.

Part II

REIMAGING EDUCATIONAL DELIVERY

3

A System Perspective on Scaling High-Impact Practices in Higher Education

AUDREY HOVANNESIAN AND
KEN O'DONNELL

ABSTRACT

Through collective impact of internal system stakeholders and external partners the California State University (CSU) Office of the Chancellor initiates and sustains numerous pilot projects to test for effectiveness and scalability across their system. The Preparing to Scale High-Impact Practices (HIPs) project was one such pilot project designed as a multicampus effort to determine a method for implementing high-impact practices in the CSU system. This project tested the efficacy of the *Fullerton model*, which engaged campuses in a four-step implementation process aligned to the Plan-Do-Study-Act (PDSA) model. At its conclusion, the project's findings indicated a multicycle PDSA approach, termed the Fullerton model in this project, is a beneficial method of scaling HIPs in higher education.

The California State University (CSU) Office of the Chancellor has supported the expansion of high-impact practices (HIPs) such as learning communities, service learning, undergraduate

Audrey Hovannesian and Ken O'Donnell led development of this work in their roles with the California State University system office.

research, supplemental instruction, and peer mentoring in a number of ways, most recently through the CSU Graduation Initiative and the chancellor's allocations for Academic and Student Success programs ($7.2 million in 2013–2014 and each subsequent year).[1] As the system accumulates evidence of HIP benefits for student learning and success, campuses are making their longstanding commitments to these practices more explicit. For example, they are creating universal freshman learning communities or requiring service learning of all students in the sophomore year.

CSU Fullerton is noteworthy for building into its strategic plan a commitment that every enrolled student will experience at least two HIPs before they graduate. To realize this goal, the university created new administrative structures—including changes to student electronic records, structures for professional development, and routines of institutional research and assessment. All of these changes were intended to create mutually reinforcing activities designed to integrate HIPs into the university culture and to demonstrate what they add to a student's college experience.

From this work, the "Fullerton model" of scaling HIPs emerged. The Fullerton model is a four-step process to prepare campuses for large-scale HIP implementation. The steps include:

1. Form a HIPs task force comprised of individuals who are key to scaling HIPs.

2. Create a campus-wide HIP inventory.

3. Identify existing HIP data and data collection practices.

4. Create structures within student electronic records to better track HIPs.

The emergence of this model was timely as it was developed just as other institutions of higher education within the CSU system, and nationally, were beginning to seek to deliver effective interventions and practices that serve a large number of students from a wide variety of backgrounds and need levels. In addition to its timeliness of creation, the Fullerton model emerged during a period when funding became available through a state systems transformation grant from the Bill & Melinda Gates Foundation to provide start-up funding for the project. This national initiative involved public university systems from a dozen states and focused on improving educational outcomes for underserved students through system-led change initiatives. The CSU Office of the Chancellor applied for this funding by designing a multicampus project, the Preparing to Scale High-Impact Practices project (HIPS project), which created a practitioner learning community to test the implementation and practicality of the Fullerton model. The Gates Foundation awarded the CSU Office of the Chancellor $200,000 for this short-term (eight-month) project. In addition, the CSU Chancellor's Office matched the grant funding to create a total project budget of $400,000, designated for project participant meetings, supplies, project management, evaluation activities, and small campus stipends for participation.

PREPARING TO SCALE HIGH-IMPACT PRACTICES PROJECT

Looking back on the work undertaken through the transformational system grant, it was identified that the successful scaling effort followed a path similar to the improvement science model developed by Langley and colleagues (2009). The HIPs project was initially guided by the four-step Fullerton model. By the conclusion of the project, the scaling methodology bore a striking resemblance to Langley and colleagues' (2009) two-step approach:

1. Identify three fundamental questions that drive the need for improvement.

2. Follow the Plan-Do-Study-Act (PDSA) cycle of improvement.

Originally named the PDCA cycle, for Plan-Do-Check-Action, or the Deming Wheel, this cycle for learning and improvement was introduced in the United States in 1986 and was abbreviated to the PDSA in 1993. Later, Langley and associates (2009) adapted the PDSA in relation to improvement science. First applied to healthcare and automotive industries, improvement science emerged from a two-part model designed to accelerate improvement. The two parts include identifying three fundamental questions that drive the need for improvement and the PDSA cycle, which tests improvement in real work settings. The PDSA cycle guides the test of a change to determine if the change is an improvement.

To support change and improvement, the CSU Office of the Chancellor often engages numerous campuses in pilot or practitioner learning communities to determine best practices to scale programs to their diverse 450,000-student population. CSU practitioner learning communities are comprised of any number of the 23 CSU campuses spanning the entire state of California, with project participation ranging from 5 to 15 campuses. Campus participation is often determined via an application process and committee decision.

The emerging "practitioner learning communities" term is somewhat synonymous to professional learning communities (PLC) or networked informed communities (NIC). The practitioner learning community also incorporates the Carnegie Foundation for the Advancement of Teaching's Six Core Principles of Improvement. The Fullerton model's parallels to the model of improvement science and Carnegie Core Principles of Improvement proved relevant and consistent throughout the project.

Improvement Science Part 1: Three Fundamental Questions

The improvement science two-part model begins by identifying three fundamental questions. The questions guiding the HIPs project were:

1. Is the Fullerton model an effective implementation method for scaling HIPs on CSU campuses?

2. Are participating campuses prepared to scale HIPs?

3. How can the CSU system further support efforts to scale HIPs?

With these questions guiding the process, a request for proposal (RFP) was issued to all 23 CSU campuses, followed by an invitation to an informational webinar on August 19, 2014. In conjunction with RFP creation, the CSU Office of the Chancellor identified a part-time (20 hours per week) project manager. The project manager, Audrey Hovannesian, a CSU alumna and assessment and student success coordinator from the CSU San Bernardino campus, assisted on initiating the project with Ken O'Donnell, senior director of the CSU Office of the Chancellor Student Engagement and Academic Initiatives and Partnerships department. The RFP outlined project requirements for joining the practitioner learning community as well as the support that participating campuses would receive for travel, meetings, and other expenses realized in connection with this work, plus an unrestricted allocation of $10,000 in recognition of their participation during the 2014–2015 academic year. Fourteen campuses addressed the following questions in short (500- to 1,000- word) applications due in September.

1. What makes this a good time for your campus to undertake work like this? Examples include other needs for institution-wide reflection, such as an impending accreditation self-study, or the beginning of a new strategic plan, or new energy behind campus priorities to improve retention, close gaps, or reduce time to degree.

2. Which three to four high-impact practices do you suspect your campuses will want to support in this way? That is, which HIPs seem to be already at large scale, relatively unambiguous to define, and prominent in the university's reputation and self-image? Which ones may already have ready evidence of measurable benefits, relative to an appropriate control group?

3. What expertise do you believe you would contribute to the group?

4. What do you most want to learn from your peers?

The selection process. Applications were submitted by designated project leads at each campus with declared support by the vice president of academic affairs, the vice president of student affairs, the head of institutional research, the head of information technology, and the chair of the academic senate. Application information was aggregated and sorted—a process that uncovered a number of similarities of responses to the four application questions. When responding to the first question related to timing, nine campuses identified that they were currently involved in an external (Western Association of Schools & Colleges) accreditation cycle, or HIPs were already deeply embedded in campus culture. Eight campuses cited current work to create systems to track HIPs, while seven campuses discussed actively engaging in the strategic planning process. Other, less frequent, responses related to campus work to identify HIP measures, needing a HIP assessment structure, current changes in student demographics, and new administration.

Applicant campuses were also asked to identify current campus HIPs. Nine campuses reported implementing service learning; eight campuses identified undergraduate research; seven campuses identified first-year experience; and the remaining campuses less frequently identified internships, mentorship, and writing intensive courses. When asked to share their specific HIP expertise, seven campuses identified assessing HIPs and HIP tracking systems as strengths; six campuses claimed expertise in scaling HIPs; and the remaining campuses identified unique HIP programs, development of HIP curriculum, HIP programs for specific student demographics, and acquiring HIP external funding as areas of expertise.

Finally, applicants responded to the benefit of joining the HIPs project practitioner learning community. Nine campuses discussed needing help in assessing and tracking HIPS, while the remaining campuses were interested in clarifying HIP definitions, scaling HIPs, and HIP-related professional development.

A selection committee of campus and system representatives was formed to evaluate the proposals. Eight campuses were selected to join the project as "pilot partners," while the remaining six campuses were designated as "network partners." The eight pilot partner campuses included Chico State University, Humboldt State University, CSU Monterey Bay, Cal Poly Pomona, CSU San Bernardino, San Francisco State University, CSU San Marcos, and CSU Stanislaus. Network campuses were CSU East Bay, San Jose State University, Fresno State University, CSU Bakersfield, CSU Channel Islands, and CSU Dominguez Hills.

Though network partners did not participate in the pilot activities, they were provided with information and project progress. Once notified, pilot partner campuses were immediately invited to gather at the annual Indiana University/Purdue University (IUPUI) Assessment Institute. This nationally recognized conference was an ideal location to begin the project due to the conference focus on assessment and effectiveness. Organizers of the conference were interested in the Preparing to Scale HIPs project and offered to share meeting space as part of their designated "HIPs Assessment" track. Thirty-one participants from the eight pilot partner campuses attended the IUPUI Assessment Conference and a project kickoff dinner meeting. By the conclusion of the IUPUI conference and dinner, project participants attained a better understanding of project timeline and they committed to the project's deliverables.

Members of the original CSU Fullerton HIPs Task Force also attended the IUPUI event and shared their experiences of creating and initially implementing the model. Pilot partner participants were given an opportunity to ask questions of the project manager and CSU Fullerton team. Most questions related to task details and concerns regarding the short timeline. Despite initial apprehensions, all campuses met the project tasks and requirements shared in the next section.

Improvement Science Part 2: Implementing the PDSA Cycle

As discussed previously, a main thrust of this project was to attempt to scale HIPs across the CSU system through use of the Fullerton model. This model, grounded on the Plan-Do-Study-Act (PDSA) cycle, proved to be an effective tool at the system and campus levels to work through change efforts that can stall as a result of tensions that can arise between administrative and academic divisions over timeline and thresholds of evidence. The second step of the improvement science model is to implement the PDSA cycle. This cycle tests changes in real work, or in the context of this project, educational settings. The PDSA cycle guides testing of change to identify whether the change is an improvement. The following steps show how the model was used to implement the HIPs project.

Step 1: Create a HIPs task force. The CSU system sent pilot partners an email, in which the first project task or step of the Fullerton model, creating a HIPs task force, was introduced. This step entailed identifying their HIP task force name (campuses were encouraged to be creative), task force members (names and titles), and their HIP inventory list (comprehensive campus HIP inventory).

Partner campuses demonstrated many consistencies to the Fullerton model in creating their HIPs task forces. Consistencies included forming task forces of about 15 (project task force membership ranged from 7 to 18) key stakeholders for implementing HIPs (i.e., representatives from administration, institutional research, institutional technology, the registrar, and HIP coordinators and directors). Project partners' feedback included the slow process of getting faculty involved, controlling the size of the task force, considering a smaller executive task force, engaging groups and individuals already involved with HIPs or other student success initiatives, and considering including student representatives. According to project partners, HIP task forces would remain in effect after the conclusion of this project to better identify, scale, track, and determine effectiveness of HIPs.

Step 2: Setting aims—HIPs in strategic plans. Setting aims is key to the PDSA cycle since improvement requires setting goals that are measurable and have clear timelines. Aims also define the specific population of patients (in this educational context, students) or other systems that will be affected. Although this project did not specifically address setting aims, the emerging practice of including HIP outcomes in campus strategic plans does identify time-specific and measurable goals or aims of implementing HIPs. CSU campuses individually create strategic plans approximately every five to seven years. Recently several campus strategic plans have included HIP implementation goals, outcomes, and action plans. Examples of CSU HIP strategic plan goals include:

- CSU Fullerton's (2013) second goal is: "Improve student persistence, increase graduation rates university-wide and narrow the achievement gap for underrepresented students." One objective of this goal is to increase student "participation in HIPs and ensure that 75% of CSUF students participate in at least two HIPs by graduation."

- CSU San Bernardino (2015) describes student success as providing "learning experiences to promote student success, achievement and academic excellence and prepare students to contribute to a dynamic society." To achieve this goal, "all undergraduate students will participate in at least three High Impact Practices (HIPs) by graduation starting with the fall 2015 cohort of incoming first-year students, preferably including one HIP within the context of each student's major."

- San Diego State University (2013) "will continue to focus on Student Success by emphasizing high-impact practices that produce transformational educational experiences and by fostering an institutional culture that recognizes and rewards student achievement."

It is speculated other CSU campuses would identify how best to implement HIPs within strategic plans. The system will continue to follow their progress and looks forward to action plan progress reports.

Step 3: HIP inventory analysis. The measure and analysis portion of this project was completed through an exploratory process to determine HIP measures currently in use by campuses. This exploratory process was necessary since consistent HIP metrics do not currently exist. Establishing measures is an integral step in the PDSA cycle to determine if a specific change actually leads to an improvement.

To identify HIP measures, project partners engaged in a number of activities, including:

- Reviewing the initial set of HIPs identified by Kuh (2008)

- Reviewing characteristics of HIPs as determined by Kuh and O'Donnell (2013)

- Convening diverse groups to brainstorm HIPs

- Identifying which HIPs are currently tracked in electronic records (all project partners use PeopleSoft)

- Coding HIPs to enable tracking in student electronic records

- Beginning to track HIPs in electronic records

Project partners also identified several possible metrics for assessing HIP effectiveness. These metrics included HIP participants'

GPAs, retention and graduation rates, engagement, and other forms of qualitative and quantitative data collected internally by HIP programs. Campuses identified systemic items requiring attention prior to implementing campus-wide HIP data tracking. According to pilot partners, the lack of centrally collected data, data collection processes (i.e., card swipe), and proper data analysis resulted in difficulty identifying the effectiveness of HIPs. Campuses are now investigating ways to consistently track data by instituting smartphone apps and swipecard technology to collect participation information and to facilitate communication with offices of institutional research to discuss data analysis protocols. Cal Poly Pomona designed an inventory of HIP programs for institutional research offices to assist in identifying how and where data are tracked in the hope of increasing communication and collaboration. Questions on the inventory include:

- Define the program in which your students participate.

- How are students assisted by your program?

- What impact are you trying to make?

- What do you think is the best measure of success of your program?

- What do students need to do to be considered active? How long? How is participation verified?

- How are you storing data? How far back does it go?

- How can we pull/gather your data? Do you get regular reports or data dumps? From where?

Campuses also investigated alternate software to better track HIPs. Seventeen of the 23 CSU campuses submitted service-learning student participation data into S4 software. S4 was originally designed by CSU Monterey Bay and is supported by a full-time coordinator. CSU San Francisco employs a similar software, Co-Mesh. Both programs function as risk management compliance data warehouses, but added features such as document and image upload are expanding function capabilities, allowing for types of activities and possibly levels of engagement to be tracked as well. S4 and CoMesh, in addition to other external and internal software, are being viewed as possible homes for co-curricular transcripts.

Co-curricular transcripts will be designed to record students' participation in co-curricular HIP programs to demonstrate their full academic experience.

Selecting changes: Select HIPs to scale. The PDSA cycle allows for participants to become actively involved in developing ideas for change. As explained previously, ideas may come from the insights of those who work in a system, on a campus, or within a HIP program, or they may come from change concepts, other creative thinking techniques, or borrowing from the experience of others who have improved. Pilot partner campuses borrowed from the Fullerton experience of identifying a method to scale and strategically implementing, tracking, and analyzing HIPs. The Fullerton model concluded with the identification of five HIPs that the campus would commit to scaling, funding, and supporting. Those HIPs were undergraduate research, freshman programs, supplemental instruction, study abroad programs, and residence halls. Although pilot partner campuses were able to identify a narrowed number of HIPs that demonstrated positive effects on measures such as GPA, graduation, and retention, many project campuses determined that more efforts to better track and analyze HIP effectiveness were needed prior to identifying signature campus HIPs as Fullerton did. CSU Chico and CSU San Marcos have employed a color-coded key to identify which HIPs are most trackable or require further analysis. They have designated levels of priority to their HIP inventory and plan to explore systemic solutions to HIP data tracking and overall implementation.

TESTING CHANGES, IMPLEMENTING CHANGES

The Preparing to Scale HIPs project illustrates the PDSA cycle step of testing changes in a real work setting—by planning it, trying it, observing the results, and acting on what is learned. This approach is the scientific method adapted for action-oriented learning. It is the hope of the CSU system to continue testing the Fullerton model and subsequent models created by Fullerton and other CSU campuses to determine an effective method for implementing HIPs.

CSU Fullerton has continued to enhance the Fullerton model by training faculty and staff to enrich and grow their identified HIPs for preparations to scale to their 37,000 students. They have designed a smartphone app to record student participation data and streamline methods of tracking and analyzing data. Their current efforts are reflective of the Implementing Change step that follows testing a change on a small scale, learning from each test, and refining the change through several PDSA cycles. As in PDSA cycles, the Fullerton team in collaboration with the Preparing to Scale HIPS pilot partners have implemented the change on a broader scale.

SPREADING AND SUSTAINING CHANGES: NEXT STEPS

The final step of the PDSA cycle is spreading and sustaining changes. After successful implementation of a change or package of changes for a pilot population or an entire unit, the team can spread the changes to other parts of the organization or in other organizations. It is proposed that future projects to scale HIPs or other changes within higher education employ a multicycle PDSA approach. This project is a demonstration of two successful PDSA cycles. The first occurred at the CSU Fullerton campus, and the second was a larger pilot for the Preparing to Scale HIPs project. As mentioned in the discussion of implementing changes, PDSA is a process requiring several iterations to determine best practices for implementation and change. With this iterative process in mind, the CSU system convened pilot partners for a culminating meeting at the end of the eight-month project. Pilot partners presented campus-specific examples of each of the Fullerton model steps and worked collaboratively to design next-step proposals to continue their HIP implementation work.

Important to the process of sustaining HIPs is the realization of the dynamic, imperfect, and incomplete nature of the work. Through trial and error, the system office and campuses quickly realized that the work of adopting, implementing, and scaling HIPs is a continuous effort. Our capacity to benefit students through HIPs will only continuously improve with a tireless focus. Without such a commitment, HIPs are just as likely to regress as they are to progress. Therefore, all models are designed to determine best practices, common metrics, and effectiveness of designing, sustaining, tracking, and assessing HIPs. This project was a catalyst to develop implementation practices, priming campuses to continue to better define, develop, sustain, track, and assess student success programs.

CHAPTER 3 TAKEAWAYS

• High-impact practices (HIPs) are evidenced practices that augment traditional learning activities and are proven to positively impact student success in diverse sets of students.

• HIPs can be resource intensive and systems allow for them to be scaled across multiple campuses, reducing some resource costs and increasing co-learning among institutions.

• Develop a vision for HIPs as a tool for improving student success.

• Create a task force with champions responsible for implementing HIPs.

• Conduct a campus-wide HIP inventory.

• Identify existing data and data collection practices.

• Develop students within student records to officially track engagement with HIPS.

• Use that data to track impact.

REFERENCES

California State University, Fullerton. (2013). *Strategic plan 2013–2018: Goal 2.* http://planning.fullerton.edu/goal2.asp

California State University, San Bernadino. (2015). *Strategic plan 2015–2020: Goal 1: Student success.* https://www.csusb.edu/strategic-plan/goal-1-student-success

Kuh, G. D. (2008). *High-impact educational practices: What they are, who has access to them, and why they matter.* Association of American Colleges & Universities.

Kuh, G. D., O'Donnell, K. (2013). *Ensuring quality and taking high-impact practices to scale.* Association of American Colleges & Universities.

Langley, G. L., Nolan, K. M., Nolan, T. W., Norman, C. L., & Provost, L. P. (2009). *The improvement guide: A practical approach to enhancing organizational performance* (2nd ed.). Jossey-Bass.

San Diego State University. (2015). *Student success updates.* http://go.sdsu.edu/strategicplan/student-success-updates.aspx

4

Embracing Disruption and New Educational Models to Transform Learning across Higher Education Systems

HOUSTON D. DAVIS AND MYK GARN

ABSTRACT

The traditional roles and paradigms of higher education systems and institutions are being challenged in an environment fraught with change, particularly as the era of the post-traditional student emerges. Diverse students with increasingly varied needs are seeking out networks of institutions that use multiple learning modalities to accelerate and reduce the costs of attaining a quality degree or credential. In recognition of this, the University System of Georgia (USG) has undertaken efforts to redesign itself to better reflect the needs of the students of today and the future. Through its USG New Learning Models 2030 Taskforce, the system supported its institutions in the creation of a new business model by facilitating the development of a shared framework for student success by harnessing data, integrating technology and learning platforms, and looking to the future to identify emergent opportunities to meet student needs. This has resulted in a system of institutions better

---

Houston D. Davis and Myk Garn were key leaders in this work during their time with the University System of Georgia.

able to change lives through student success, making them more sustainable in the process.

> Disruptive innovations within the higher education enterprise require that we think critically about current strategies and position our university and college system for the challenges and opportunities that will come in the next decade. The USG and its institutions must remain proactive to stay abreast of the rapidly changing world of public higher education.
>
> —University System of Georgia Strategic Plan (2013)

Higher education is in the midst of turbulent change. An academic culture steeped in reflection, exploration, and interaction is being disrupted and reconstructed into a globally connected ecosystem of networked teaching and learning tools. Roles and paradigms held dear and true are challenged by models where teacher and student roles blend to become 24/7 co-creators and co-learners. The rate of change and unpredictable, unrelenting emergence of new, disruptive models makes planning and preparing for the future even more conflicted, confusing—and critical.

This scenario was the challenge facing the University System of Georgia (USG) in 2013. A recently completed report on the system's distance learning needs had surfaced many critical needs—but few visionary directions—for the system to plan from or consider. This need was clear to Chancellor Hank Huckaby in November 2013 when he addressed a convening of the system's leading educational entrepreneurs at a symposium entitled "MOOCs and Beyond" (Huckaby, 2013). Challenging the leaders to examine and explore the future fearlessly, he stated, "We don't know what lies beyond," which he acknowledged as both okay and important to innovation. This observation framed and guided the system initiative and Georgia's intent to "invent the beyond."

THE NEED FOR NEW THINKING AND NEW STRATEGIES

The University System of Georgia, with 318,000 students and 29 institutions ranging from research universities to access-oriented state colleges, has made degree completion a top priority. The state of Georgia is committed to increase to 60 percent by 2025 the percentage of working-age adults holding a postsecondary degree or credential. Achieving this goal is critical because of the significant shift in demand for degrees in the state and national workforces. In 1973 a high school graduate in the United States could expect to be educationally prepared for 72 percent of jobs in the economy. By 2018 that figure was projected to have decreased to 38 percent (Carnevale et al., 2010).

Some form of education and training beyond high school is becoming a baseline requirement for participation in the knowledge economy. In Georgia, 1.1 million citizens between the ages of 25 and 64 have some college but no degree. Many of those former students are just like the students who are in our classes right now—in good academic standing but a life circumstance away from dropping out. Another one million Georgians have a high school diploma but no prior enrollment in postsecondary education opportunities and represent some of the most at-risk citizens moving forward in an economy firmly rooted in what you know and can do.

Business as usual will not allow us to meet the education attainment goals required by the current and emerging US and global economies. Ensuring that the pace and scale of the transformation needed is within the tolerance and ability of the stakeholders to grasp, embrace, or endure is critical to the future of Georgia. To continue its leadership role, the system must identify future trends and opportunities that both inform its current plans and catalyze the development of new ones. Over the next 15 years, higher education will accelerate the transition from a culture of an eighteenth-century memory-based, industrial teaching model to a twenty-first-century social model of networked learning and co-creation.

Exploring, enabling, and ensuring success in new delivery models has many dimensions, but student success and quality of teaching and learning must be at the center of our work. As higher education nationally grapples with change, there is an opportunity for USG to be a leader in using new content and delivery strategies such as scaled, higher enrolled courses and expanded open educational resource content for high-quality, more affordable academic course and program opportunities for Georgia students. Committed to partnering with other sister systems, USG can share in lessons learned and benefit from scale of strategy and implementation. By being a leader, USG can insist on the preservation of academic quality and find appropriate ways to use these tools to increase access, improve affordability, and shorten time to degree. Georgia is viewed as a state and system that is well positioned to deliver, yet the model showing elements of the ecosystem that surrounds our teaching and learning strategies (figure 4.1) reveals the complexity of the challenge, whether in traditional classrooms or via the newest educational technology tools.

From the outset of this work, it was recognized that USG had made good progress or functionality in networks. Additional work is needed in delivery systems, student support, and mobile deployment, but a foundation is in place that is on par with the best nationally. Strategies for deploying affordable resources, assessment, and analytics require additional work, are less mature, and require greater progress, but the USG is firmly committed to developing these tools to meet faculty and student needs. Identity management and financial models are the least developed and are core components of the exploratory work that is underway on how new models of delivery will shape our system of institutions.

Figure 4.1. The University System of Georgia Student Success Ecosystem

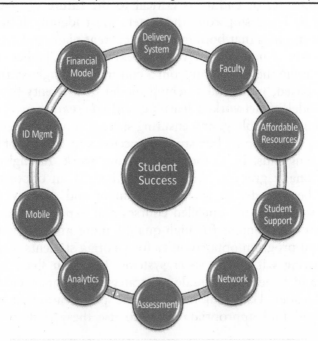

If the system is to be successful, institutions must provide multiple pathways and educational experiences to meet the needs of students and the state. It is certainly reasonable for Georgia residents to expect that USG has university and state college opportunities that afford access, residential, and selective experiences. Indeed, these pathways and educational experiences complement, influence, and contribute to the quality of our system of higher education.

Whatever the numbers associated with the overall degree completion goals or considerations of current teaching and learning strategies, all require us to focus on:

1. Meaningful degree opportunities for students that have value in the economy and for advanced learning

2. Bridging gaps to degree completion for capable students who are at risk of dropping out or have already dropped out

3. More efficiency with our resources to include all categories of budget resources but also resources such as effort, concern, opportunities, and choices

4. USG as the major driver of the knowledge economy—educationally, economically, socially, culturally—and committed to cutting-edge higher education leadership

NOT NOW . . . NOT NEXT . . . BUT AFTER NEXT

In the world of academic innovation there are many experts and experienced entrepreneurs who know what needs to be done next to improve faculty and student success in the rapidly changing environment of academe. New models can be a significant challenge to our core enterprise and the academic, financial, and physical space assumptions that the majority of our enterprise is built upon. It is difficult to break free from these lenses and challenge the power of what needs to be done now—and next.

More bandwidth, more funding, more professional development, more attention to quality and security are all very important but also can be unhelpful when one is tasked with visioning not what should come next—but what will come *after* next.

Figure 4.2. The University System of Georgia New Models Foci (circa 2013)

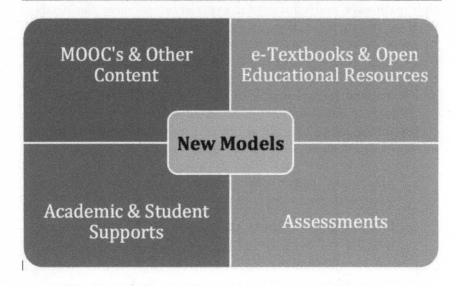

THE USG NEW LEARNING MODELS 2030 TASK FORCE: COAUTHORING THE FUTURE OF EDUCATION

In September 2014, the system created the New Learning Models 2030 Task Force (NLM 2030). With a membership of 65 thought and opinion leaders, the task force brought together a broad, representative swath of USG stakeholders. From presidents, provosts, faculty, students, and staff, every one of the system's institutions was represented by at least one stakeholder. This assembly of the system's "best and brightest" was asked to envision and chart a future path for higher education in Georgia.

The charge to the NLM 2030 was to catalyze and build a more informed framework of future possibilities and strategic options. Scenario planning begins with a focus: an issue or idea that is at the heart of the matter (Schoemaker, 1995). The focus is important because it helps to narrow the possible futures to those that will help lead us to better decisions. For its activities, the NLM 2030 focused on the future of higher education in 2030 setting out to:

- Build a shared framework for strategic thinking that encourages diversity and sharper perceptions about change and opportunity for the University System of Georgia.

- Identify and analyze trends, uncertainties and critical success factors that will impact higher education instructional and business models over the next fifteen years.

- Generate and evaluate strategic options that extend the breadth, depth and understanding of how new, nascent and future technologies and trends will impact and can benefit, and should be leveraged by, the system.

- Identify, assess, and recommend new business logic and models that promise success for emerging markets, stakeholders, and innovations.

- Use these findings to generate and evaluate strategic options to guide planning for, and increase the system's ability to meet, the needs of all academic stakeholders in the year 2030. (NLM 2030, 2016)

Because predicting the future with any certainty is wholly unsatisfactory, the NLM 2030 chose a scenario-based planning process—not to predict the future but to visualize a range of possible futures and reflect on how prepared the USG was for them. Scenario planning helps to make the driving forces at play in a market sector visible and, by developing them into scenarios with multiple possibilities, planners can anticipate a wider range of challenges, opportunities, and outcomes (Schoemaker, 1995).

Scenario-based planning increases the ability of stakeholders to envision future possibilities and challenges in volatile and unpredictable markets that are beyond the immediate, predictable horizon. These explorations build a shared approach and conceptualization of future needs and opportunities for USG, ensuring, encouraging, and supporting more effective and cohesive transformations. The resulting frameworks are authentic and internally valid, communicating the challenges and opportunities facing the system and the critical success factors and strategic options the system might employ in planning for the future.

*Crowdsourcing the Future: How to Invent and Explore
the Beyond*

Because "new models" means new methods of learning, NLM
2030 used online tools and models to conduct and complete a
scenario-based planning project. While the task force comprised the
core stakeholder group of 65 individuals, access and participation
in the planning activity was expanded to the entire system and to
academic systems, institutions, and stakeholders across the United
States through the "Invent the Beyond" (ITB) and "Explore the
Beyond" (ETB) massive, online, open-stakeholder collaborations
(a twist on MOOCs) that overlaid the activities, experiences, and
deliberations of the broader task force.

Use of the open-stakeholders collaborative format (fall 2014
and spring 2015 "courses" were offered via the Brightspace Open
Courses) enabled the task force to work collaboratively and communicate regularly without the need to convene as frequently and
to dramatically increase the number (over 500 individuals participated in the ITB and 194 in the ETB MOOCs) and distribution
of stakeholders contributing to and informing the scenario building
and planning processes (figure 4.3).

Figure 4.3. Comparison of Stakeholder Participant Percentage between NLM
2030 and Invent/Explore the Beyond MOOCs

Stakeholder Community	New Learning Models 2030 Taskforce (n=65)	Invent/Explore the Beyond MOOCs (n=500+)
Higher Education Administrators	87 %	23 %
Faculty	8 %	42 %
Students	5 %	23 %
Other		12 %

The ITB online collaborations used crowdsourcing to develop future scenarios and to explore and describe the factors critical to the success of students, faculty, and postsecondary institutions in 2030. The more than 500 participants were asked to determine:

- What factors will be critical to the success of the university system and its stakeholders over the next 15 years?

- What new learning practices and business models will best guide and support learners, faculty, and institutions in and to 2030?

During the fall 2014 ITB course, interacting through the structured online environment, participants identified and quantified the driving forces and critical uncertainties facing higher education over the next 15 years. They used those critical uncertainties to establish candidate matrices for scenario development, wrote "headlines for the future," selected the final matrix, and then developed four robust scenarios for the future of learning in 2030.

In spring 2015, ETB course participants identified the critical success factors for student, faculty, and institutional stakeholders, evaluated the pressure to change current instructional services that institutions provide to students and teaching activities that faculty employ, and determined the implications that new learning models would put on institutional functions and how they would need to change—by 2030. The final capstone session for both collaborative courses recapped and consolidated the learnings and implications of the complete process, resulting in a set of critical success factors and a framework for informing institutions and individuals as they build their future plans.

Driving Change

The USG scenario-based planning process (figure 4.4) began by identifying and prioritizing the primary drivers of change (economic, technological/instructional, social/cultural, and policy/political) as perceived by three primary stakeholder groups: students, faculty, and institutions. Those issues impacting the future whose trajectory is relatively certain (e.g., rising operational costs) became categorized

Figure 4.4. The University System of Georgia Scenario-Based Planning Process

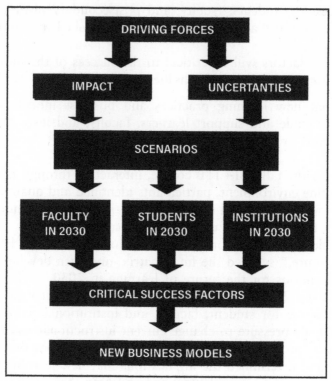

Adapted from Shoemaker, 1995

as "trends" and helped undergird the development of the scenarios. Drivers that were highly uncertain, where the degree and type of impact is unpredictable (e.g., legislative mandates), became the variables from which the differing narratives of the USG scenarios would be crafted.

The task force rated over 70 change drivers in terms of the potential impact each driver might have on the future and the degree of certainty or uncertainty of that impact on the system and its stakeholders. The resulting 30 most impactful and uncertain drivers were then presented to the ITB course participants for their input. Using both implicit and tacit knowledge, the most impactful and uncertain drivers were then combined and weighted into general clusters of "key driving factors."

By determining the polarities for each factor (e.g., a faster pace of change vs. a slower pace of change) and then creating a matrix based on the two most-voted informative drivers, the task force constructed a matrix (figure 4.5) of four different possible views of the future for higher education between 2015 and 2030. In this case, the NLM 2030 process identified the two key uncertainties as "Sources of Learning," with polls labeled "Closed/Academy" and "Open/Open Source/Co-Created," and "Pace of Change," with the polarities of "Rapid" and "Managed/Slow."

Figure 4.5. Final Candidate Set Presented as a Matrix

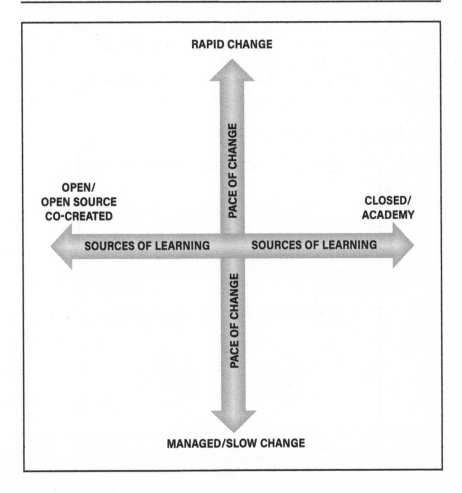

From Critical Uncertainties to Scenarios

Using the critical uncertainties that form our matrix as reference points, the next step was to fill out the story of the future: How did it happen in this particular way? What had to happen first in order for us to get to this future? What else is going on in this future given the critical uncertainties? During the narrative development process, the "other" uncertainties—the 29 that did not end up in the matrix—were used to provide a much deeper sense of what the future would be like in a specific scenario. For example, in a future where the pace of change is rapid and most learning is from open, noninstitutional sources, what would the public funding model be for higher education? What would the state of the national economy be? Answering these questions from the context of our critical uncertainties uncovers nuances in the futures that help to make them both distinct from other scenarios and sufficiently rich to serve as valuable planning tools.

Finally, each scenario (figure 4.6) was given a name to be used as a shorthand for what the conditions of that future are. The names

Figure 4.6. Final Invent the Beyond Matrix

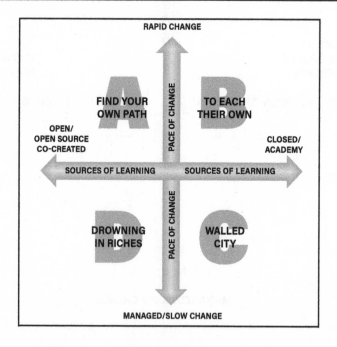

should evoke the overall feel of the scenario and help someone who may not be familiar with the process or the steps taken to arrive at this future understand the underlying pressures and conditions that define the scenario. For example, the "Find Your Own Path" scenario connotes learners (and faculty) who must chart their own course through an unruly world.

Exploring the Scenarios

The four USG 2030 scenarios co-developed by the NLM 2030 and the ITB course participants provide four very different future narratives that higher education stakeholders can use to populate and plan for possible futures. By "populating" each of these scenarios with avatars for the three stakeholder groups, the taskforce was able to identify the critical success factors necessary for each of these communities to thrive and succeed in 2030—and the implications for new learning and new business models that the system will need to invent and implement to support its students, faculty, and institutions.

Presented next are tables (4.1–4.4) showing the uncertainties driving each scenario (sorted into four change driver categories of social, technological, economic, and political) and representative cameo content from each scenario narrative.

In the world of Find Your Own Path (table 4.1), change is the only constant, institutional prestige is devalued, the "wisdom of crowds" is interpreted through algorithms and predominates as the truth, data is destiny. In this world, analytics, algorithms, and machine learning have triumphed. Apps now know how to make sense of the world well enough that most people do not care if a recommendation comes from a person or a program.

Information is everywhere, published by people and by programs. The world seems to seethe with change, and it is fast paced. Many people feel that the pace creates constant disruptions—if not on the grand scale, at least on the personal scale. There seems to always be something new to learn, something new to adapt to, something—from devices to skills—that has become obsolete.

In higher education, institutional prestige has been devalued. Value now resides in the ability to meet the needs of the individual,

Table 4.1. Planning Scenario 1: *Find Your Own Path*

Find Your Own Path
Rapid Change—Open Source/Co-created

Social	*Technological*
• US-centric global perspective • Education is inexpensive and accessible • All music is world music • Just-in-time skill learning augments lifelong learning models (higher education buy-ins) • Well-respected content = credibility • Highly transparent social structure and behaviors	• Attention management systems help people organize information networks to meet needs • Technology displacement of labor • There are games for everything • Online portfolio systems replace transcripts and resumes/CVs • Rapid obsolescence and the need to relearn models and acquire new skills • Internet is free and fast
Economic	*Political*
• Vibrant world economy • Fewer trade barriers • International brands, many emerging from new markets • Situational results drive perceptions of value • Wide-ranging employment issues arise as more and more labor is replaced by automation	• US government actively reinventing itself • Movement toward more direct democracy • Weak public sector • Pragmatic decision-making • Pressure for new definitions of "value" and "worth" becomes political issue

fueled by the collective "wisdom" of the crowd. The power of a degree is diminished as workplaces shift to micro-degrees and endorsements. The cost of "learning" plummets.

Leading-edge educators are working with learning apps to embed their own approach to learning and critical thinking within the recommendation and analysis engines. These educators offer subscriptions to their "personal takes" on the world, which differentiates them from more generic, open-source analytics.

The landscape of To Each Their Own (table 4.2) is one where higher education institutions have pushed back and closed ranks in the face of the unrelenting pace of change. Higher education now competes directly with business, using its size, scope, and position to block out external partners from trespassing on its patents, proprietary practices, and intellectual property. Educators, researchers

Table 4.2. Planning Scenario 2: *To Each Their Own*

To Each Their Own	
Rapid Change—Closed/Academy	
Social	*Technological*
• Educators viewed as entrepreneurs • Education is expensive, but work programs make it reachable • Strong East Coast/West Coast bias • End of interleague sports leads to East/West championship battles • Technology-driven isolation from standards fragmentation	• Rapid innovation and new technologies adopted within • Technologically savvy educational institutions "colonize" less tech-savvy schools • Strong commercial space programs led by research programs
Economic	*Political*
• Higher education establishes strong position on patents, proprietary practices, and intellectual property, often acting more like businesses than schools • Credentials are essential passports to opportunity • Only the biggest of businesses can keep up with pace of change • Poor management practices lead to greater organizational dysfunction	• Business and education carve up political clout leading to new battles and new gridlock • Courts and regulators fail to manage increasingly proprietary "standards"

in particular, who are now seen as entrepreneurs, take models of academic-economic cooperation to new heights.

Protecting the investment on research and development does not imply a slow transfer of technology but rather a new competitive model where higher educational institutions share less among one another as they seek to convert their intellectual property into economic value.

The pace of change is fierce. Organizations that cannot keep up, including many universities and colleges, get subsumed into larger structures. "Embrace change or be eaten" is a common mantra. However, rapid mergers and acquisitions have led to increasingly dysfunctional management practices that often fail to find the right balance in the chaotic environment. Multiple cultures and multiple infrastructures slam into each other at light speed, but management has little time to weave a new, cohesive culture. When it comes to teaching, nothing is sacred because if it is not relevant, then it does not count, and that means anything old that has not found a way to prove relevance has been swept away. Credentials and affiliations are the essential passports to opportunity. The economic gap between those with credentials and those without widens.

In the Walled City (table 4.3), stakeholders find comfort in a more "livable" pace of change—but with anxiety over an environment somehow out of sync. Slow change means a slower economy with fewer opportunities for the ambitious. Tight restrictions and control on social, economic, and technological advances reinforce and extend social, cultural, and political ossification. That said, the slow pace of change also means government promises get fulfilled before they get derailed or obsoleted by new technology. Academe

Table 4.3. Planning Scenario 3: *Wallked City*

Walled City Slow Change—Closed/Academy	
Social	*Technological*
• People feel overmanaged and underachieved • Resurgence in book publishing • Education institutions touted as the saviors for a world of underachievement • Traditional journalism returns (but not distributed in traditional ways) • Highly supplemented higher education tuition	• Technology feels stale • Because technology is not changing as fast, mastery of all forms of technology are at an all-time high • Automation focuses on tracking negative political movements and other insurgencies
Economic	*Political*
• Stagnant global economy • Business is seeing long-term bets pay off, albeit at subpar performance rates • Significant reductions in election costs as people have more time to actually engage in issues (advertising declines)	• Tight political control on change facilitated by industrial and social engineering • Reputation of government generally improves • Middle East continues to devolve as United States pulls out to focus on domestic policy • Ideas about what facts should be vs. actual facts predominate government decision-making

is seen as the arbiter of knowledge and skills, and institutions guard this power closely. Strategic alliances between institutions and private industries consolidate this power and encourage targeted innovation toward specific objectives. Educational institutions have found that for many classes, applying the industrial method is working well. They create cookie-cutter classes with clear, measurable outcomes and franchise them out.

The cost of education is high, but it has stabilized as the external sale of courses and the monetization of staff lead to new sources of income. With the costs of adapting to rapid change no longer a constant business cost, institutions and individuals can make other strategic investments, some to bolster their status (either as gatekeepers for institutions, or as individuals), others to extend their mission or interests.

The Drowning in Riches (table 4.4) scenario delivers what today's stakeholders think they want: a controlled pace of change.

Table 4.4. Planning Scenario 4: *Drowning in Riches*

Drowning in Riches Slow Change—Open Source/Co-Created	
Social	*Technological*
• Educational systems have lost control of their marketplace • People cobble together learning from a variety of sources • "Being social" replaces "being on social media" • Personal and local newsletters, blogs, and other online media proliferate	• Technology adoption in academia is very slow • High distrust of automated solutions and "Big Data" • Bring-Your-Own-Device common • Ease of publishing and consumption • Technology is powerful but isolated as coordination and collaboration wanes • Social media falters
Economic	*Political*
• Lack of resources to transform information into value • "Information" labor jobs offer secure employment and upward mobility • Poor quality information increases accidents and leads to major industrial disasters	• Chaotic political systems as new political movements emerge, but most do not get broad traction • Business is equally disjointed in its leadership position as slow growth has left a vacuum of industrial leadership • Elected leaders have plenty of sources from which to choose their "facts"

There was a time when people trusted computers for everything, and they started to automate all manner of human endeavor from creating shopping lists to driving cars. The Great Attack stopped all that. Over a period of a just few weeks, hackers raided many major financial institutions. Billions of dollars simply disappeared.

Public funding for education is on the wane, along with tax dollars being taken in by the federal, state, and local governments. The generally stagnant economy makes obtaining funds from other sources difficult. Some companies, however, are sitting on piles of pre–Great Attack cash hordes and offer funding to institutions that can offer specific research assistance or a particular hedge.

In this scenario students cannot turn to any single source to complete their education. Institutions remain stuck in a model that no longer meets the needs of their students or the workplace. They turn inward, reflecting on their lost stature, which further deteriorates their motivation for change.

HIGHER EDUCATION IN 2030

In the four possible scenarios for students, faculty, and institutions developed through the USG's scenario-based Invent/Explore the Beyond process, change drivers, trends, and uncertainties were extrapolated and explored to develop the critical factors these higher education stakeholders will need to be successful over the next 15 years. Asked to examine all four scenarios for the essential themes and implications to describe the challenges and opportunities for these communities, the NLM 2030 framed four central insights to guide development of the next strategic actions the University System of Georgia must undertake.

1. **The lines between learning and living will become increasingly blurred.** In 2030 students will need to take greater control and responsibility for finding, funding, and managing their educational experience. As new populations grow and enter the higher education pipeline, they will increasingly be blending work, family life, and studies. For these students, the system must increase the options for student learning and accommodate transforming lifestyles.

2. **Pressure will increase to control costs, increase access, and ensure success.** In 2030 some intuitions will look very different.

To stand out, some will focus on excellence in niche domains; others will incorporate, and even evolve into, new ways of doing business. In the USG, all institutions will need to increase access, affordability, and flexibility in the academic marketplace.

3. The changing nature of work in America drives changes in higher education. Successful institutions will balance the values of a traditional education while reinventing themselves as career-building and sustaining opportunities. Partnerships with the prospective employers of USG graduates will start sooner, extend long past graduation, and be much deeper overall. Growth of contingent workforce models will create opportunities to increase ongoing and persistent alignments between college and career.

4. Faculty members have different relationships with colleges. The disruption of traditional roles and need for empowered academic entrepreneurs will only increase. Faculty will be more active in building partnerships and ensuring the continued growth of the institution. To succeed in 2030 the system will need to evolve with and empower the changing cultures of the campus.

RECOMMENDATIONS OF THE NEW LEARNING MODELS 2030 TASK FORCE

While the Invent/Explore the Beyond initiative framed USG's challenges and provided some clarity to perceptions of ambiguity, ultimately the USG and campus leadership must move from this universe of possibilities and isolate the primary issues and actions that will follow. From the four broad implications, six critical areas emerged where the task force felt there was urgency for action. These six critical areas were pursued, with a roadmap for priorities in distance education, system technology infrastructure, academic program and personnel priorities, and new delivery model development.

1. Our technology infrastructure has to support new learning models. As a system, Georgia's universities and state colleges are going to be very purposeful about making certain that we are focused and strategic with regard to investments in the teaching and learning technical infrastructure. The system has many pockets of innovation. At the campus level, there are colleges and departments that are declaring a desire to be innovative and try new things. These academic and support units need to have the policy space and the encouragement that give them room to explore, innovate, and test assumptions. This approach is balanced with the need for the system to be very purposeful as it turns its attention to the future, including prioritizing its technology and learning support during times of scarce resources. USG must leverage educational technology to enable efficiencies and ensure quality of all programs.

For example, throughout the system significant conversations and planning are underway around competency-based education (CBE) and its possibilities. CBE may require new and/or highly modified technologies including student information, financial aid, learning management, and customer relationship systems. If every institution begins to develop its own solutions—all we end up doing is splintering attention and inefficiently investing in a fractured approach to the techno-structure. Instead, leadership needs to make certain that our system-level information technology services (ITS) and their campus partners are building solutions together with the principles of flexibility and utility. Thus, future projects will be scoped to support single-campus initiatives as well as multi-institutional, cooperative projects.

2. The system needs to centralize administrative functions for critical distance education assets. In addition to the innovators' needing space and support, the task force encouraged the system to continue to grow existing assets, turning them into opportunities for even more Georgia citizens. A key high-profile asset is eCore, the system's online, collaborative general education coursework available to students at every institution. Pairing eCore with an emerging strategy to collaborate on degree completion options, known as eMajor, creates a virtual eCampus strategy to respond to calls to leverage scarce resources toward high-quality, affordable educational opportunities.

To ensure that institutions have the financial and human resources to respond to ongoing needs for rapid changes, the USG needs to strengthen the strategic alignment of institutions with system initiatives, while at the same time eliminating policy and process barriers to degree progression and completion. To increase the options of instructional models available to Georgia students, the USG will establish a centralized USG competency-based education unit that will identify and coordinate a set of comprehensive, system-level, CBE services, resources, and infrastructure. All USG institutions will have access to these capabilities to develop and deliver their own and/or collaborative CBE programs.

3. The fiscal environment needs to include new business models, including tuition pricing and financial aid. It is against this backdrop of new learning models and their impact on our current practices that USG is finding multiple business model challenges. The new business models include addressing tuition pricing and financial aid in a way that ensures a price point that allows affordability and quality to provide value.

What inventing and exploring the future showed the USG is that very powerful things are going to happen with or without us. What the Georgia campuses must do is use their considerable collective weight as a system to make certain that USG is proactive in having some impact on those changes. Therefore, the Georgia system has made fiscal policy in support of new delivery models a priority as we look to the future.

To address this need, the USG will identify and address processes, policies, and regulations that prevent the flexibility and adaptability that the system and its institutions will require to be successful in 2030. It will explore and propose fiscal models that increase affordability and allow autonomy and fiscal control, while enabling new pedagogical models to be effective and cost efficient for both students and institutions.

The system is also taking very seriously accreditation concerns that represent a critical policy nexus of these changes. The regulatory environment for regional accreditation around these new business models is evolving rapidly. The system is partnering with regulatory players to find the balance between their regulatory framework and our goals as a system and single institutions. Experience in governance reveals that it is easier to invite those counterparts to the table during planning and development—rather than to *surprise* them with implementation.

4. The system will continue to encourage and fund the use of affordable instructional materials and textbooks. Students want the highest-quality educational experiences available to them, but markets are increasingly demanding that these opportunities be deployed in ways that are sensitive to and minimize student debt.

The USG must pursue next-generation learning modalities that promote high-quality access experiences and integrate open educational resources and course/program redesign.

Through the Affordable Learning Georgia (ALG) project, the system is helping faculty integrate more open educational resources into their courses and into programs of study. To date, approximately 150 faculty systemwide are leading a rethinking of how textbooks and other learning objects are used in courses. Through the collective efforts of this first phase of ALG, the system has identified $13.5 million in textbook savings that are being enjoyed by our students in FY2016. Another $2.5 million for textbook costs was avoided in the current year by the eCore courses moving toward an open-source textbook model.

5. New and coordinated delivery strategies for high-demand degrees are needed. The system is committed to the creation of affordable postsecondary educational options and degree programs that address student needs and marketplace demands. In addition to continuing support of a broad range of educational programs, the system will focus on areas that have labor shortages as well as high-demand degrees and credentials and invest in learning paths and delivery methods that are cost effective. This strategy should emphasize helping students gain the skills and experience they need to join the workforce in their desired field of endeavor, serving the broadest range of students effectively and at the lowest possible cost.

To achieve this goal, the USG committed to creating and aligning stackable credentials and delivery methods with distinct career opportunities to help students gain the skills and experience they need to join the workforce in their desired field of endeavor. In part this approach is a recognition that all our institutions form a coordinated network for delivering postsecondary education. It provides a great opportunity for an institution to be the anchor school, coordinating a network of two or three other campuses that are jointly offering a degree at an affordable price point for Georgians. It will also coordinate and expand college and employer partnerships that blend apprenticeships, reimbursement plans, and cooperative experiences with concurrent associate's and bachelor's degree programs.

Currently the system's previously mentioned eMajor approach is an emerging and evolving example of this type of leadership and collaboration. Here the system will provide new learning design and support strategies to priority programs, recasting the current strategies to include certificates, associate's degrees and bachelor's degrees, or options that maximize credits and ensure more flexible opportunities for returning adults.

EMPOWER THE CHANGING CULTURES OF THE CAMPUS

Throughout their year of work, the NLM 2030 task force continually emphasized the importance of faculty development and faculty supports as USG looks to the future. All these prospects for change affect not only the curriculum but also everything that surrounds that curriculum. The system must support, enable, and expect leadership from the faculty networks throughout the USG.

The institutions and the system will need to continually identify and adjust to shifts in regulatory approaches to ensure the balance between centralized and localized leadership. USG should lead in ways that increase flexibility in faculty roles and compensation models that respect, reward, and accommodate both traditional and emergent models of teaching, research, and service.

The system will propose strong professional development support for faculty to stay current, thrive as lifelong learners, and expand knowledge of entrepreneurial possibilities. It will develop "risk-to-reward" frameworks to guide faculty members about viable research opportunities and increase possibilities for promotion and tenure to include credit for engaging in "high-risk" innovative activities. Finally, it will address the role of adjunct and contract instructors in accomplishing the instructional, research, service, cultural, and governance goals of the institution.

CONCLUSION

The strength of the University System of Georgia is that we have 29 institutions—each with its own mission, role, and scope to provide a rich set of educational access opportunities. Although the campuses have unique footprints, they weave together a tapestry that creates a statewide "campus" that is formed by the borders of the state of Georgia, and our collective campus community is the 10.5 million people who live inside of the state of Georgia. We know that we can better serve our public with more flexible, affordable, and quality educational offerings, and technology and innovation will open up those possibilities.

At the onset of the NLM 2030 visioning project, the USG needed to know how well positioned Georgia's research, teaching, and service assets are against the challenges that the state and system will face. All participants in the project were challenged to consider what the higher education future might look like. While not necessarily focusing on what that future might look like for any particular institution, the consensus led to trends, challenges, and opportunities that will require the collective system to make strategic and calculated actions to pursue the greatest priorities—whether for what is next or after next.

CHAPTER 4 TAKEAWAYS

- University System of Georgia embraced the mantra "invent beyond" to keep the system and campuses focused on looking to the future.

- Scenario-based planning increases the ability of stakeholders to envision future possibilities and challenges in volatile and unpredictable markets that are beyond the immediate, predictable horizon.

- Learning is increasingly everywhere and around the clock. There will be movement to blending of work, family, and studies.

- Systems can advance learning innovations through supporting new shared technological infrastructures, centralizing administrative supports, exploring new revenue models, and incentivizing development of high-need academic programs.

REFERENCES

Carnevale, A. P., Smith, N., & Strohl, J. (2010) *Help wanted: Projections of jobs and education requirements through 2018.* Georgetown University, Center on Education and the Workforce. https://cew.georgetown.edu/cew-reports/help-wanted/

Huckaby, H. (2013). *MOOCs and beyond: Remarks from the chancellor* [Video file]. http://www.completegeorgia.org/MOOCS_and_Beyond_Videos

New Learning Models 2030 Task Force (NLM). (2016). *NLM mission.* http://afternext.completega.org/Mission

Schoemaker, P. J. H. (1995). Scenario planning: A tool for strategic thinking. *Sloan Management Review, 37*(2), 25–40.

5

PREDICTIVE ANALYTICS AND CHOICE ARCHITECTURE AND THEIR ROLE IN SYSTEM-SCALE STUDENT SUCCESS

Empowering a Mobile Advising Tool across Campuses

TRISTAN DENLEY

ABSTRACT

In an effort to improve educational attainment across the state of Tennessee, the Tennessee Board of Regents, a system of 6 universities, 13 community colleges, and 27 colleges of applied technology, has engaged in systemwide change efforts, with the system office moving from an accountability role to acting more as a resource and support for innovation. To illustrate this approach, four projects are discussed that are emblematic of how predictive analytics and data-mining technology, coupled with research findings from fields such as behavioral economics, can combine to create strategic insights into the structure of the system as a whole and how students succeed and fail. These projects are also emblematic of how those strategic insights can be used to inform changes to system policy, as well as broad-scale system initiatives.

Tristan Denley was the architect of the work described in this chapter when he worked for the Tennessee Board of Regents.

Virtually every enterprise taking place today at the Tennessee Board of Regents (TBR) system office and at each of our institutions is centered on improving student outcomes. Governor Haslam's Drive to 55 initiative, the Tennessee Higher Education Commission's strategic plan, and the Complete College Tennessee Act have all articulated the relationship between economic growth and the legitimate aspirations of the state's two public higher education systems. The interplay between governmental and higher education entities is crucial to achieving the state's overall objective of 55 percent of Tennesseans earning postsecondary credentials by 2025.

For the TBR system office, this objective meant that the focus was on empowering staff and institutions to engage in activities that promote the ongoing success of more students. While traditionally TBR has been a system primarily focused on compliance and accountability, we have more recently refocused on finding ways to partner with and empower our institutions to do the work of change. The result is an evolving redefinition of the relationship between the system and its institutions. Our interest is less about regulating and more about helping each institution meet its goal of increasing relevant, high-quality results. In this environment, the goal of the system is to help our institutions create processes and frameworks for continuing evaluation and to identify interventions that might help improve the outcomes of any given strategy. We are dedicated to helping identify and develop best practices and then to supporting efforts to scale those practices across the system and beyond, while moving from being perceived as a roadblock to being a resource.

To this end, within the system we have used a variety of styles of convenings to share lessons learned and build systemwide capacity and momentum across a variety of constituencies. These meetings range from the formal decision-making of our board meetings and quarterly sub-councils, to strategy planning Completion Academies involving campus leadership teams, to a variety of sessions with faculty groups and functional groups. Convening in these ways is crucial to this work. Only by bringing together groups of faculty and campus leaders from across the system can the conversations take place that allow all roles to feel professionally valued and involved in the work.

While a broad array of initiatives is unfolding across the system, all efforts revolve around a central axis. We aim to create an educational environment that enables students to effectively find an educational direction that leads into their career, to equip that direction with a clear pathway of study that plots out their coursework to graduation, and to use technology to inform both students and their advisors about how to steer and adjust that pathway along the way. The system and member institutions, through ongoing discussions, are working together to create the policy, incentive, and resource structures to bring this change about.

As illustrative of this approach we will discuss some specific initiatives in more detail. These four projects are emblematic of how predictive analytics and data-mining technology, coupled with research findings from fields such as behavioral economics, can combine to create strategic insights into the structure of the system as a whole and how students succeed and fail. These projects are also emblematic of how those strategic insights can be used to inform changes to system policy, as well as broad-scale system initiatives.

ACADEMIC FOCUS

The process through which students navigate institutions from admission to graduation involves large numbers of crucial decisions. Despite the advantages to having a clear direction of study (Jenkins & Cho, 2012), one-third of first-generation students nationally begin college without identifying a major or program of study, whereas only 13 percent of their peers with college-going parents do not declare a major upon enrollment (Chen & Carroll, 2005). Students often select their majors with little information about what is involved in successfully completing the program and often discover too late that the picture they had of that discipline is very different from the reality (Kirst & Venezia, 2004; Smith & Wertlieb, 2005). Low-income and minority students express less knowledge of programmatic demands than their peers. Although students may think that they have an interest in a particular area, they have often received little information about whether their academic abilities create a realistic chance of successfully completing that program. What is more, they may associate each discipline with a limited number of careers and often eliminate disciplines from their list of choices because those jobs are unappealing, without realizing the true variety of career opportunities that lie on the other side of graduation.

Information and choice clearly have a significant impact on a student's ability to navigate through a degree successfully, which significantly raises the stakes on the ways in which the information is presented and how the choices are framed. Schwartz (2005) has argued for a "paradox of choice"—that having too many options can lead to a "decision paralysis." Tversky and Kahneman have carefully analyzed how decisions are made in the face of an abundance of choice (Kahneman, 2011; Kahneman & Tversky, 1979; Tversky & Kahneman, 1974). They, and others, have found that when presented with too many choices people fall back on a variety of rules of thumb or anecdotal evidence, or they rely on cognitive ease and the halo effect. Often, poorer choices are made in situations of an abundance of choice, using these fallback methods, than in situations with more limited choices. In fact, the literature on "choice overload" suggests that too many options can result in several adverse experiences, including a depletion of cognitive resources and post-decision feelings of regret (Reed et al., 2011; Schwartz, 2005). Given the multiplicity of choices entailed in selecting from a college's array of majors or programs, and then satisfying the curricular requirements, these adverse experiences may play a significant part in student success, especially for at-risk populations. In fact, it seems that a more focused choice structure would be far more effective and preferred (Diamond et al., 2014; Reed et al., 2011; Schwartz, 2005). Once again, underrepresented minority students and first-generation students, who often do not have the tools to sift through the superabundance of information, are the most at risk for this adverse effect.

To explore the initial impact of how students go about choosing their degree programs, we carried out a careful analysis of TBR systemwide data. We chose to examine student persistence over a period of three academic years for those students who began without a chosen program and see how their choosing might correlate with their persistence. Of the 4,470 students in the study, 57 percent completed all three years, however that percentage was dramatically affected by program choice or lack thereof. Only 29 percent of the students who did not select a program during their first year completed all three years, compared to a persistence rate of 95 percent of students who did find a program during their first year. In fact, more than half of those students who arrived in our system not enrolled in a specific program (undecided) dropped out before choosing any particular program.

This systemwide analysis suggested that student success would be enhanced if we were able to enable more students to identify a direction of study as early as possible. The behavioral economics research on the effects of choice paralysis suggested, however, that we would need to create a modified choice architecture for these students in which they could initially select from a smaller number of possibilities (Sethi-Iyengar et al., 2004; Shah & Wolford, 2007) rather than requiring them to choose one program from the full array of possibilities. Through discussions involving academic leaders and faculty groups across institutions, we worked together as a system to create nine *academic foci* that would act as a guiding structure for student choice. Once in place, those students who were not ready to decide on a specific program could instead choose to begin one of the nine focus areas. By appropriately structuring their initial courses, we could craft semesters of study so that all the coursework would satisfy academic requirements for all the programs in that focus area. These curated semesters would allow students to feel that they were studying what they had chosen (Jenkins & Cho, 2012) while also enabling them to refine their choice to a specific program. The criteria for this work did not involve restructuring colleges and departments, but rather identifying a collection of affinity groups of disciplines that together encompassed all the programs at all 19 community colleges and universities, while intentionally recognizing that a single degree program might readily be found in several foci simultaneously.

We agreed on eight—applied technology, arts, business, education, health professions, humanities, social sciences, and STEM—and retained a ninth exploratory general education focus to create a direction for students who were initially unable to identify with any of those other eight possibilities.

Figure 5.1. Nine Academic Foci of Student Choice at Tennessee Board of Regents Campuses

HEALTH PROFESSIONS
APPLIED TECHNOLOGY
STEM
HUMANITIES
GENERAL EDUCATION
BUSINESS
SOCIAL SCIENCES
EDUCATION
ARTS

As a system we have now implemented these academic foci as part of the program choice architecture. Every incoming student in 2015 began in either a specific program or an academic focus. No student was classified as undecided or defaulted into a general degree classification. Each institution has developed enhanced orientation and advising initiatives to ensure that students were able to make more informed choices about the future possibilities that each of these programmatic pathways opens up. They have also developed first-year curricular experiences for each focus area that allow students to take coursework that applies to each of the disciplines within that focus and enables students to refine their choice to a particular program of study.

To analyze the initial student perception of this experience we surveyed the incoming 2015 student class with a broad academic mindset instrument. While we hope the data from the over 6,000 replies will provide significant insights into student attitudes toward their college experience, the data do provide an initial window into the effectiveness of this new choice architecture. When asked why they had chosen their program, focus, or major, overwhelmingly (78%) students said that they had chosen an area in which their interests lie. Of the remaining students, they expressed motivations connected with salary, parental suggestion, or a role model. Less than 1 percent expressed that their choice had been motivated solely by the requirement to "pick something."

Further time and analysis will be necessary to assess the long-term effects of structuring student program choice in this way, but these initial data suggest that members of 2015's incoming class have overwhelmingly begun their studies along a defined pathway.

Figure 5.2. Students' Reasons for Program or Focus Choice at Tennessee Board of Regents Campuses

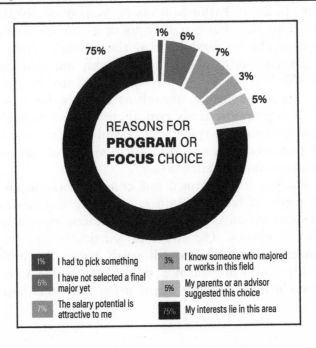

COURSE REVITALIZATION

A system as diverse as the Tennessee Board of Regents needs to offer a vast array of coursework as part of all of its programs of study. In fact, each semester the system's roughly 200,000 students study over 8,000 different courses. However, more than half of the million student-course enrollments lie in around 30 of those classes. This observation in no way implies that the other 7,970 courses have no role to play, or that we need far fewer courses—if anything, we probably need more. But it does point to a peculiarity of curricular structure: Course enrollment is highly concentrated.

Over the last 15 years there has been a growing understanding of the structure of complex networks (Albert & Barabási, 2002; Watts & Strogatz, 1998). These *small-world networks* can be used to analyze a wide range of systems in nature, technology, and societal phenomena from the World Wide Web to virus spread. One feature of this type of network is the existence of *hub* vertices—nodes in the network with an overabundance of connections. These hubs play a disproportionately large role in the connective structure of the overall network, both enabling effective flow around the network and fragmenting the network when they are damaged or removed (Albert et al., 2000; Pastor-Satorras & Vespignani, 2001).

By studying the course transcripts of graduates across the system we were able to establish that the system's course structure is itself a small-world network. The highly enrolled classes that comprise the lion's share of the enrollment are the hubs in this network. But consequently, as well as being highly enrolled they also play a disproportionately critical curricular role in the overall learning structure of the system: Successful learning in those classes disproportionately leads to further success; lack of success in those classes leads to failures elsewhere.

This analysis has informed our course revitalization initiative in which teams of faculty members at system institutions develop new and more effective pedagogies for exactly these most curric-ular-impactful classes. The structural curricular analysis suggests that changes in these classes will reach across the student body very quickly and will influence success across the sweep of the curriculum. In fall 2016, we began using this same logic as part of understanding how best to increase accessibility to instructional materials for students with disabilities.

Beginning in fall 2013, we invited teams of faculty members from across the system to propose a reenvisaged structure for one of these highly impactful classes on their campus. They were asked to propose a new approach, together with a proposed assessment structure, with the intention that they would be able to establish that in this new format more students would learn more material more deeply, and consequently would be more successful in that class. Support was to be provided for the successful teams from funds provided by the system office, as both recognition and incentive for the work to be done. We had over 120 team proposals and were able to fund 50 projects spanning the curricular spectrum. The selected teams implemented their pilots and collected their data during fall 2014. The projects involved over 14,000 students and 160 faculty members at 18 campuses, in courses from 16 disciplines. Faculty members designed new course structures from the full spectrum of contemporary techniques, including supplementary instruction, learning communities, and flipped and hybrid classroom models, as well as using technologies in a variety of learning settings.

The projects fell into two broad categories—33 of the projects were revitalizations of standard gateway classes, and 17 were revitalization projects that were part of our systemwide pilot of co-requisite remediation. Those we will discuss in the next section.

The purpose of these pilots was to identify successful new pedagogies. While not every new approach was as successful as planned, 21 of the 33 projects produced results with increased student success rates in comparison with their comparator groups. That increase was statistically significant, often strikingly so, for 12 of those projects. Twenty of the projects took their new model to a broader scale in fall 2015. We will continue to gather data about the success of those scaled projects, as well as identify ways in which the system can help provide support or pathways to overcome roadblocks that would enable this work to scale yet more fully.

In fall 2014 we also invited a new set of proposals, and another 50 projects—nine of which are fully online courses—were piloted in fall 2015. We are also exploring ways in which system resources could be used to enable successful pilot work to be scaled when there are insufficient campus resources to do so.

CO-REQUISITE REMEDIATION PILOT STUDY

Work has been underway for more than a decade to impact the success rates of students who begin their postsecondary studies in developmental education. Despite that nationwide effort, the success rate remains shockingly low (Complete College America, 2012). Figures (American Association of Community Colleges, 2014) show that around two-thirds of the students entering community colleges each year are required to take at least one developmental class before they are able to enroll in credit-bearing work. The overwhelming majority, however, does not ever complete the credit-bearing classes for which they are being prepared. In fact, fewer than 20 percent of students who place into developmental mathematics complete a college-level mathematics course within three years (Bailey et al., 2010).

It is not that remediation is an ineffective experience, or that students do not pass remedial courses, but there are richer phenomena at work. As many as 30 percent of these students do not attend the first course or subsequent remedial courses or drop out along the way. Further, 30 percent of those students who complete their remedial courses do not attempt their gateway courses within two years (Complete College America, 2012; Jenkins et al., 2009).

The work so far has largely focused around improving the proportion of students who successfully complete remediation, but more recent work has instead focused on a unified approach that knits together the credit-bearing and remediation experience. In 2007, as part of a systemwide redesign project funded by the Fund for the Improvement of Postsecondary Education (FIPSE) and the National Center for Academic Transformation, Austin Peay State University pioneered an approach to remediation for incoming students who arrive with developmental needs in mathematics, reading, and/or writing. This *co-requisite model* transformed Austin Peay's previous success rate of fewer than 10 percent of students completing a credit-bearing math class over several semesters to more than 70 percent completing a credit-bearing math class in a single semester.

This work has been recognized by the Dana Center, Complete College America, Education Commission of the States, and Jobs for the Future as a national model for success in developmental education.

Based on this initial work, the TBR system began a study of the effectiveness of the systemwide approach to developmental education in community college, when success was viewed from the perspective of students completing a credit-bearing math, writing, or reading-intensive class within an academic year. To understand more clearly how the preparedness of students would affect their potential success in these course completions, we chose to disaggregate the data by ACT sub-score. Since systemwide in Tennessee, just as nationwide, more than 60 percent of TBR students begin college with a need for remediation in math, reading, and/or writing, the results of the analysis were startling. Overall, only 12.3 percent of the students who began in a remediation course completed a credit-bearing mathematics class, and only 30.9 percent completed a credit-bearing writing class. When disaggregated by ACT sub-score, the success rates of these students did vary, but only one in four or five students on the cusp of having college-ready scores successfully completed a credit-bearing math class in an academic year (see figure 5.3).

Figure 5.3. Historical Percentages of Community College Students Completing a Credit-Bearing Math Class in an Academic Year

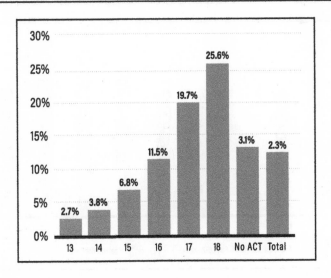

In fall 2014 and spring 2015, we carried out a substantial pilot of the co-requisite model of instruction in the community college setting. In mathematics, 1,019 students (645 in the fall and 374 in the spring) across nine campuses were enrolled directly into an introductory statistics class and were required also to attend a supplementary instruction experience. Similarly, 957 students (393 in the fall and 564 in the spring) at seven community colleges were enrolled into a credit-bearing freshman writing class with required co-requisite support. We disaggregated the data by ACT score so that we would be able to gauge the effectiveness of this approach for students with various levels of preparation.

The results of the pilot were extremely encouraging and strikingly consistent between the two semesters. In mathematics, of the 1,019 enrolled students, 63.3 percent received a passing grade in the class (compared to 12.3% under the old model) (see figure 5.4). Not only did we see this 51-percentage-point increase overall, but we saw strikingly higher success rates for students at every ACT mathematics sub-score.

These successes were not limited to mathematics. Of the 957 students enrolled in the writing pilot, 60.9 percent received a passing

Figure 5.4. Completion of Gateway Math Course by Student ACT Sub-score: Community College Prerequisite model versus Co-requisite Pilots

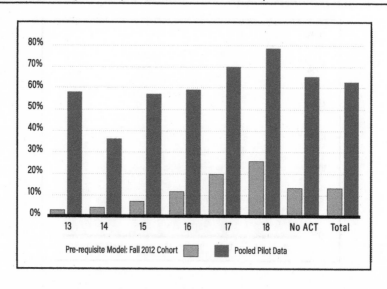

grade in the class. Once again this result compares extremely favorably with the historical success rate of 30.9 percent, and once again we saw gains for students at every ACT writing sub-score (see figure 5.5).

Recent discussion concerning the affective and noncognitive aspects surrounding the college remediation experience recognizes the profound impact of students questioning whether they belong, recognize the purpose of their study, and believe that they are capable of learning the material (Farrington et al., 2012; Hulleman & Harackiewicz, 2009; Silva & White, 2013; Yeager & Walton, 2011). We compared the success rates for students enrolled directly into the credit-bearing classes with the historical rates of students successfully completing the remediation designed to prepare them for that class (see figure 5.6). We have shown the results for mathematics here, but the results for writing are similar. Once again, significantly larger proportions of students at every ACT sub-score level completed the credit-bearing class in a single semester than traditionally have completed their remediation in a full academic year. These results add significant credence to there being more than academic effects involved in remediation success.

Figure 5.5. Completion of Gateway Math Course by ACT Sub-score: Community College Prerequisite model versus Co-requisite Pilots

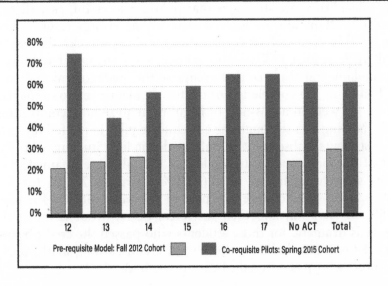

Figure 5.6. Community College Math: Completion of Prerequisite Model
Learning Support versus Completion of Co-requisite Pilot Gateway

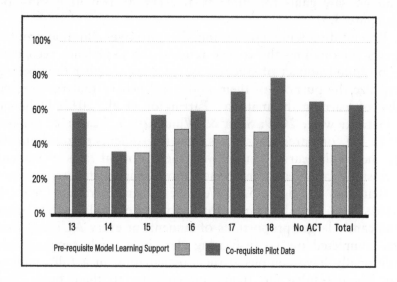

In response to this body of new data, the system organized three
co-requisite academies in March 2015, inviting faculty from all 19
institutions to present results from their pilot models and develop
plans to take their pilots to full scale. These convenings were crucial
as a vehicle to share strategies that proved successful, as well as to
share important lessons learned that would inform future expansion of this approach and identify major roadblocks that would
need to be resolved. They also refined a system understanding of
the fundamental features that comprise this pedagogical approach.

Following the completion of the first academic year of implementation, we were in a position to begin to analyze how completing a
credit-bearing class through the co-requisite pilot in the fall impacted
those students' subsequent overall academic life. Students who were
part of the math and writing pilots in the fall were retained to the
spring semester at higher rates (72.1% for math, 77.1% for writing) than those who were not part of the pilot (68.5% for math,
66.5% for writing) and their historical peers. What is more, that
change is dramatic for those students who passed the credit-bearing
class (84.6% for students who passed credit-earning math, 83.4%
for those who passed credit-bearing writing).

The students who took part in the co-requisite pilot also had a much-increased fall-to-fall retention rate compared with their colleagues who went through standard learning support. The retention rate for the co-requisite students was 57.4 percent compared with 43.3 percent of the more than 38,000 who were not part of the pilot. There was increase in retention, no matter whether the student passed his or her credit-bearing math class in the fall, but the increase was most pronounced for the students who successfully passed their credit-bearing class compared with their colleagues who completed their remediation. For these students, the increase was from 47.3 to 68.5 percent. These results are similar to other implementations of the co-requisite model in other systems and institutions (Complete College America, 2016).

All TBR universities and community colleges began fully implementing the co-requisite mathematics, reading, and writing models for all students beginning in fall 2015. Although there is much yet to analyze in the semester's data, we can already see that the initial improvements promised by the pilot are apparent.

Overall for those students who took a co-requisite mathematics class in fall 2015, 51 percent received a passing grade in their credit-bearing mathematics class in that first semester (see figure 5.7). This represents a more than fourfold increase over the original

Figure 5.7. Community College Math: Completion of Prerequisite Model Learning Support versus Completion of Co-requisite Mathematics

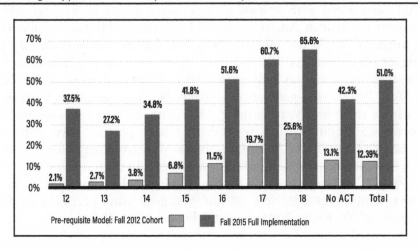

prerequisite model, in which only 12.3 percent of those students achieved that same passing grade in an entire academic year. Similarly, the pass rate for those students who took a co-requisite writing class almost doubled over the historic 30.9 percent over an academic year to 58.7 percent in a single semester.

Just as in the pilots where we saw substantial gains in student success across the full range of ACT scores, the pass rates in the credit-bearing classes were larger than the rates at which students historically completed their developmental courses in a full academic year. While these results were a little lower than we saw in the pilot data, they are still substantial improvements over the previous approach.

USING PREDICTIVE ANALYTICS

It has been a longstanding reality that success in higher education is very uneven across the population of the United States. Consistently over the last three decades, racial minority, low-income, and first-generation students have earned postsecondary degrees at substantially lower rates than their counterparts. Although the degree-attainment rates for these three groups have increased over that time horizon, those improvements have not kept pace with the degree attainment rates of students in general (Engle & Lynch, 2009; Ross et al., 2012; U.S. Census Bureau, 2006). The most recent IPEDS data show that while 49 percent of White students who began college in 2007 graduated with at least an associate's degree in six years, 37 percent of African American and 33 percent of Hispanic students graduated. While the rate at which low-income students enroll in higher education has doubled since the 1970s, the graduation rate for these students has only grown from 7 to 10 percent (Engle & Lynch, 2009). First-generation students begin to trail their peers as early as their first year, earning 18 credits, on average, compared to the 25 credits earned by students whose parents have degrees (Chen & Carroll, 2005). In fact, similar patterns emerge for minority, low-income, and first-generation students in every success metric governing student progress through college when compared with their White, higher-income, or non-first-generation peers (Engle & Lynch, 2009; Kelly, 2005; Lumina Foundation, 2013).

These attainment gaps appear to be significantly influenced by information gaps. First-generation, low-income, and minority students often do not have the advice system that surrounds students whose parents or other relatives have been to college. Information is certainly available to these students, but without knowledge of the structure and nomenclature of higher education, they are unable to even frame the questions that would enable them to become informed (Diamond et al., 2014; Hagelskamp et al., 2013).

As challenging as the factors involved in choosing the right degree program are, navigating a degree program is no less crucial or challenging. Each student must choose from a variety of courses that satisfy the requirements of their general education core and then their various degree program requirements. Ideally, students would make strategic decisions about the courses that are most likely to lead to their success. Instead, they are faced with making choices about courses of which they are not in a position to distinguish ahead of time. Indeed, higher education has been described as a "post-experience good" (Diamond et al., 2014), since not only is it difficult to envisage or evaluate the experience of studying a particular course or program before hand; the true benefits of that study may not be understood until long into the future. While advisors are often well equipped to provide valuable advice in their own field, most programs require students to take courses from across the full spectrum of disciplines, and advisors find themselves challenged to offer useful advice in disciplines far from their own. As higher education funding has become more and more depleted, even access to this advice is far from guaranteed.

Yet access to advising is vital as nationwide, on average college students take up to 20 percent more courses than are needed for graduation—not motivated by a desire for a diverse curriculum but because they had to rethink their plans several times. In an environment in which time to degree has considerable implications for a student's likelihood of graduating, a semester of extra coursework plays a crucial factor, especially for students who attend part time or for whom financial impacts weigh heavily (Complete College America, 2011).

While these educational achievement gaps have remained stubbornly present, one promising avenue of attack seems to be the use of predictive analytics to provide individualized information to each student and to his or her advisor, and so to level the information playing field more evenly (Johnson et al., 2013). Predictive analytic techniques move from a retrospective-reporting data stance toward the use of large data sets to make detailed predictions about the future. These predictive models enable strategic action to be taken in the present to potentially provide significant improvements in the future. This work is not an attempt to automate the advising function, but rather to empower it. By providing detailed, focused, and timely information to both student and advisor, we can enable the advising conversation to be a much more nuanced exchange to improve student outcomes.

While at Austin Peay State University, I was part of the initial work in this direction. The concept was to combine predictive analytics with behavioral economics to create an environment that would help students and advisors select impactful courses. We were intentional in providing an interface that neither restricts nor prescribes their choices, but instead empowers choice by creating an information source with a larger than human viewpoint and supported by data from previous choice patterns (Denley, 2012). Instead, the system, Degree Compass, uses predictive analytics techniques based on grade and enrollment data to rank courses according to factors that measure how well each course might help students progress through their programs. In their book, Thaler and Sunstein (2009) discuss strategies to better structure and inform complex choices. Degree Compass was designed with this practice in mind to create a choice architecture to "nudge" students toward course selections in which the data suggest they would have the most success, but using an interface that would minimize choice overload.

A growing body of data (Denley, 2013, 2014) now shows that this approach has both significantly increased retention progression and graduation rates at participating institutions while also cutting the achievement gaps in half for low-income and minority students. This work, together with work at Georgia State University (Renick, 2014), Arizona State University (Kadlec et al., 2013), and in the University of Hawaii (Lacro & Rodwell, 2012), shows the possible impact of this style of technology when it is combined with on-campus initiatives.

The Degree Compass work concentrated on seeing how individualized analytics can be used to help optimize course and curricular selections, but there are many other ways in which these kinds of technology can be used across higher education. Building on work that was part of the Gates Foundation State Systems Transformation Project, which ties the case studies in this volume together, we have recently developed, at system scale, a new predictive analytics technique that we call *trajectory analytics*. This methodology allows us to estimate the probability that each student has to complete the degree program in which he or she is currently enrolled. The system is also able to compare that likelihood to the likelihood they have of completing other programs at their institution and generate advantageous alternatives where possible that align with their career aspirations. The system also generates an annotated transcript showing how grades in critical classes shape that overall completion probability and triggering alerts when low grades create barriers to future success. Using this technology, which is now available at every university and community college, each institution is able to identify those students who are the most at risk of not completing their current program, initiating an advising intervention.

We have also been able to combine this approach with another mentioned earlier. By refining the methodology used to inform the strategic courses for revitalization, we have been able to also identify those courses that are most critical to the completion of each particular program at each campus. Furthermore, the trajectory analysis provides grade thresholds for those classes that significantly influence student success.

In fall 2015 we convened institutional leadership teams from every system institution for a two-day meeting at which each school made definitive plans about how its leaders might weave these and other predictive analytics technologies into the policy, procedure, and functional structure of their campus.

Our next step is to complete the deployment of an online advising interface, accessible to students and advisors through mobile technologies that will synthesize this and other strategic completion information about each student into an easy to use and simple interface. The design process for this interface involved several groups of faculty members and professional advisors, as well as groups of students who were facilitated in a human-centered design experience, and ongoing conversations across the system. That work has shown that while various campuses have a variety of student success elements, such as early warning systems and guided pathway systems, there is advantage to creating an interface in which all the available elements are seamlessly brought together for the end user.

CONCLUSION

Although we have discussed these four initiatives as separate entities here, in fact they are themselves intertwined with one another and are parts of a coordinated approach to improve student success across the Tennessee Board of Regents. Although not mentioned here, we are also exploring the influence of an array of student supports, financial aid options, and tuition structures; high-impact practices and noncognitive factors; and academic mindset, to name but a few. However, what has been discussed in this chapter illustrates some important basic principles about recent change in our system and how it has been achieved.

First, while individual innovation is crucial, as a system we are focused on creating change at scale. Only by implementing at a systemwide scale will the academic careers of sufficiently many students be affected to reach Tennessee's goals as a state. But engaging the system in broad-scale change will only be effective if the things that change truly do measurably improve student success. Consequently, we are committed to basing that change around a solid research base and to creating robust assessment and data structures that can ensure that we are able to document, measure, and guide improvements. Achieving all these goals requires a subtle balance between creating a preponderance of conclusion-drawing evidence with a timeliness that allows the work to proceed.

Change of this kind can also only be achieved by a commitment to inclusion. We have been deliberate in bringing together groups of classroom faculty members, researchers, advisors, students, and campus administrative leaders on an ongoing basis, while also meeting with groups on every campus. The conversations generated from these gatherings have been crucial to shaping the structure of these innovations and maintaining a coherence and unanimity of direction as we have moved forward, as well as allowing the dissemination of best practices as they are discovered. Only an ongoing commitment to listening, sharing, and providing resources to overcome future obstacles will bring this work to a successful conclusion.

CHAPTER 5 TAKEAWAYS

- TBR has shifted away from a tradition focused on compliance and accountability toward finding ways to partner with and empower our institutions to do the work of change.

- Systems have the capacity to scale out evidence-based practices in such a way that substantial numbers of students can be effected to meaningfully advance state and national goals.

- Meaningful and sustainable change happens through the broad engagement of stakeholders in a co-learning experience.

- System-level data provide opportunities to understand student success behaviors, patterns, and barriers across multiple campuses.

REFERENCES

Albert, R., & Barabási, A.-L. (2002). Statistical mechanics of complex networks. *Reviews of Modern Physics, 74,* 47–97. doi:10.1103/RevModPhys.74.47

Albert, R., Jeong, H., & Barabási, A.-L. (2000). Error and attack tolerance of complex networks. *Nature, 406,* 378–382. doi:10.1038/35019019

American Association of Community Colleges. (2014). *Fast facts from our fact sheet.* http://www.aacc.nche.edu/AboutCC/Pages/fastfactsfactsheet.aspx

Bailey, T., Jeong, D. W., & Cho, S.-W. (2010). Referral, enrollment, and completion in developmental education sequences in community colleges. *Economics of Education Review, 29,* 255–270. doi:10.1016/j.econedurev.2009.09.002

Chen, X., & Carroll, C. D. (2005). *First-generation students in postsecondary education: A look at their college transcripts* (NCES 2005–171). National Center for Education Statistics. http://nces.ed.gov/pubs2005/2005171.pdf

Complete College America. (2011). *Time is the enemy.* http://www.completecollege.org/docs/Time_Is_the_Enemy.pdf

Complete College America. (2012). *Remediation: Higher education's bridge to nowhere.* http://www.completecollege.org/docs/CCA-Remediation-final.pdf

Complete College America. (2016). *Corequisite remediation: Spanning the divide.* http://completecollege.org/spanningthedivide/

Denley, T. (2013). *Degree Compass course recommendation system.* Educause. https://net.educause.edu/ir/library/pdf/SEI1303.pdf

Denley, T. (2014). How predictive analytics and choice architecture can improve student success. *Research & Practice in Assessment, 9*(2), 61–69.

Diamond, A., Roberts, J., Vorley, T., Birkin, G., Evans, J., Sheen, J., & Nathwani, T. (2014). *UK review of the provision of information about higher education: Advisory study and literature review.* Higher Education Funding Council for England. http://www.hefce.ac.uk/pubs/rereports/Year/2014/infoadvisory/Title,92167,en.html

Engle, J., & Lynch, M. (2009). *Charting a necessary path: The baseline report of the Access to Success initiative.* The Education Trust. http://edtrust.org/wp-content/uploads/2013/10/A2S_BaselineReport_0.pdf

Farrington, C. A., Roderick, M., Allensworth, E., Nagaoka, J., Keyes, T. S., Johnson, D. W., & Beechum, N. O. (2012). *Teaching adolescents to become learners: The role of noncognitive factors in shaping school performance—A critical literature review.* University of Chicago, Consortium on Chicago School Research.

Hagelskamp, C., Schleifer, D., & DiStasi, C. (2013). *Is college worth it for me? How adults without degrees think about going (back) to school.* Public Agenda. http://www.publicagenda.org/media/is-college-worth-it-for-me-pdf

Hulleman, C. S., & Harackiewicz, J. M. (2009). Promoting interest and performance in high school science classes. *Science, 326,* 1410–1412. doi:10.1126/science.1177067

Jenkins, D., & Cho, S.-W. (2012). *Get with the program: Accelerating community college students' entry into and completion of programs of study.* Community College Research Center, Teachers College, Columbia University. http://ccrc.tc.columbia.edu/media/k2/attachments/accelerating-student-entry-completion.pdf

Jenkins, D., Jaggars, S. S., & Roksa, J. (2009). *Promoting gate-keeper course success among community college students needing remediation: Findings and recommendations from a Virginia study (summary report)*. Community College Research Center, Teachers College, Columbia University. http://ccrc.tc.columbia. edu/media/k2/attachments/strategies-promoting-gatekeeper-success-summary.pdf

Johnson, L., Adams Becker, S., Cummins, M., Estrada, V., Free-man, A., & Ludgate, H. (2013). *NMC horizon report: 2013 higher education edition.* http://redarchive.nmc.org/publications/2013-horizon-report-higher-ed

Kadlec, A., Immerwahr, J., & Gupta, J. (2013). *Guided path-ways to success: Perspectives from Indiana college students & advisors.* Public Agenda. http://www.publicagenda.org/media/report-guided-pathways-to-student-success

Kahneman, D. (2011). *Thinking, fast and slow.* Farrar, Straus and Giroux.

Kahneman, D., & Tversky, A. (1979). Prospect theory: An analysis of decision under risk. *Econometrica, 47,* 263–292. doi:10.2307/1914185

Kelly, P. J. (2005). *As America becomes more diverse: The impact of state higher education inequality.* National Center for Higher Education Management Systems. http://www.nchems.org/pubs/docs/Inequality%20Paper%20Jan2006.pdf

Kirst, M. W., & Venezia, A. (Eds.). (2004). *From high school to college: Improving opportunities for success in postsecondary education.* Jossey-Bass.

Lacro, E., & Rodwell, G. (2012). *Using technology to enhance the academic journey.* EDUCAUSE. https://library.educause.edu/resources/2012/5/case-study-7-star-using-technology-to-enhance-the-academic-journey

Lumina Foundation. (2013). *A stronger nation through higher edu-cation.* http://www.pesc.org/library/docs/about_us/whitepapers/a-stronger-nation-2013lumina.pdf

Pastor-Satorras, R., & Vespignani, A. (2001). Epidemic spreading in scale-free networks. *Physical Review Letters, 86,* 3200–3203. doi:10.1103/PhysRevLett.86.3200

Reed, D. D., DiGennaro Reed, F. D., Chok, J., & Brozyna, G. A. (2011). The "tyranny of choice": Choice overload as a possible instance of effort discounting. *Psychological Record, 61*(4), 547–560.

Renick, T. M. (2014). *GPS advising at Georgia State University*. Georgia State University. http://oie.gsu.edu/files/2014/04/Advisement-GPS.pdf

Ross, T., Kena, G., Rathbun, A., KewalRamani, A., Zhang, J., Kristapovich, P., & Manning, E. (2012). *Higher education: Gaps in access and persistence study* (NCES 2012-046). National Center for Education Statistics. https://nces.ed.gov/pubs2012/2012046.pdf

Schwartz, B. (2005). *The paradox of choice: Why more is less*. HarperCollins.

Sethi-Iyengar, S., Huberman, G., & Jiang, W. (2004). How much choice is too much? Contributions to 401(k) retirement plans. In O. S. Mitchell & S. P. Utkus (Eds.), *Pension design and structure: New lessons from behavioral finance* (pp. 83–95). Oxford University Press.

Shah, A. M., & Wolford, G. (2007). Buying behavior as a function of parametric variation of number of choices. *Psychological Science, 18*, 369–370. doi:10.1111/j.1467-9280.2007.01906.x

Silva, E., & White, T. (2013). *Pathways to improvement: Using psychological strategies to help college students master developmental math*. https://www.carnegiefoundation.org/resources/publications/pathways-improvement-using-psychological-strategies-help-college-students-master-developmental-math/

Smith, J. S., & Wertlieb, E. C. (2005). Do first-year college students' expectations align with their first-year experiences? *NASPA Journal, 42*(2), 153–174.

Thaler, R. H., & Sunstein, C. R. (2009). *Nudge: Improving decisions about health, wealth, and happiness*. Penguin Books.

Tversky, A., & Kahneman, D. (1974). Judgement under uncertainty: Heuristics and biases. *Science, 185*, 1124–1131.

U.S. Census Bureau. (2006). *Current population survey, October supplement, 1972–2006*. Author.

Watts, D. J., & Strogatz, S. H. (1998). Collective dynamics of "small-world" networks. *Nature, 393*, 440–442. doi:10.1038/30918

Yeager, D. S., & Walton, G. (2011). Social-psychological interventions in education: They're not magic. *Review of Educational Research, 81*, 267–301. doi:10.3102/0034654311405999

Part III

Building an Innovation Infrastructure

6

THE ROLE OF HIGHER EDUCATION SYSTEMS IN PROMOTING EDUCATIONAL INNOVATION

Developing Competency-Based Learning Environment at Scale

STEVEN MINTZ

ABSTRACT

Among higher education's most pressing challenges is to significantly increase the number and diversity of students who succeed in the high-demand fields of biomedicine, computer science, data science, and engineering. To meet this challenge, the University of Texas System's Institute for Transformational Learning and its team of curriculum architects, instructional designers, educational technologists, and data scientists has partnered with campus faculty to reimagine every facet of the learning experience. By working with coalitions of the willing on islands of innovation, the UT System is designing, testing, and rigorously evaluating new educational models for emulation across its campuses and at other institutions nationwide.

Higher education faces two profound challenges. One is to better meet the needs of a student body that consists increasingly of nontraditional and low-income students whom colleges and

Steven Mintz led the development of the initiative described in this chapter when he worked for the University of Texas System.

universities have traditionally failed to serve well. These students include first-generation college students, students from historically underrepresented groups, nonnative speakers of English, commuter and part-time students, full-time workers, and family caregivers—many of whom struggle with financial challenges, inadequate preparation, language issues, disabilities, and work-family stresses.

The other challenge is to better prepare students for the future of work in a globalized information and knowledge economy. As the economy has grown more volatile, uncertain, and complex, higher education must do a more effective job of preparing students for careers in high-demand fields that have historically had very high rates of attrition, such as engineering, mathematics, and the health sciences, while also instilling cross-cultural competencies and computational, communication, collaboration, and critical thinking skills that today's multicultural workplaces require.

At present, too many students are not acquiring the postsecondary credentials that are essential to enter a rewarding career, and too many young people lack the skills and competencies necessary to thrive in the shifting economy. To meet these challenges, institutions are rethinking the design of their curricula, embracing new pedagogies such as flipped classrooms, taking advantage of new technologies and delivery modalities, expanding internship and service-learning opportunities, and redesigning support services. Innovations abound, including summer bridge programs, learning communities, expanded undergraduate research experiences, and other high-impact practices. These experiments have moved the dial on college completion incrementally, but, clearly, new educational models are needed to get a higher proportion of students to academic and career success.

This chapter examines the role of university systems in promoting educational innovation. Today, 60 plus public university systems operate in more than 37 states, serving roughly three-quarters of all students at four-year public institutions. First established in the late nineteenth century, public university systems proliferated after World War II with an eye to reducing institutional competition for state appropriations, discouraging legislators from lobbying on behalf of particular campuses, and preventing mission creep among component campuses. Originally, these systems were responsible for establishing legislative priorities, allocating capital and operational funds, auditing campus expenditures, approving academic programs, and overseeing campus compliance with state and federal rules and regulations. In recent years, university systems have taken a more aggressive and expansive role in setting tuition and fees; monitoring and assessing campus performance; providing shared services; and coordinating relationships with school districts, community colleges, foundations, and government. But of all the roles that systems have embraced, perhaps the most striking is the growing role in promoting innovation and coordinating online learning.

Some systems, of which the most striking examples include the State University System of Florida, the State University of New York system, and the University of California system, have instituted a more centralized or coordinated approach to distance education with varying degrees of success. Others, such as the University System of Georgia, have consolidated campuses and created an electronic core curriculum, allowing students to complete their first two years of college online, with enrollment counseling, bookstore, library services, tutoring, test proctoring, and accessibility services coordinated centrally.

Among the most ambitious efforts to foster educational innovation systemwide has taken place within the University of Texas (UT) System. In 2011, the system's Board of Regents allocated $50 million to establish the Institute for Transformational Learning (ITL), to serve as a systemwide catalyst for innovation. The ITL was given a bold mandate to establish UT institutions as leaders in the development and implementation of best-in-class online and technology-enhanced learning; expand access to educational programs that will improve learning outcomes; and reduce costs for students and their families, universities and taxpayers, and promote a culture of educational innovation throughout the UT System. The institute's efforts to cut through the iron triangle of access, affordability, and student success offer a striking case study of the challenges and opportunities that state systems face when they seek to promote innovation across multiple dimensions, including curricular design, pedagogy, delivery modes, student lifecycle services, and learning analytics.

THE CONTEXT

The UT System is among the nation's largest and most diverse. Its eight academic institutions and six health institutions educate a majority-minority population of more than 216,000 students, including over 130,000 FTE undergraduate students. Forty-five percent of the system's undergraduates are African American or Hispanic, 40 percent are Pell Grant recipients, 39 percent are transfer students, and 43 percent work full time. This student population is a microcosm of the emerging demographics of US higher education—and includes the student profiles that higher education nationwide has too often failed.

The UT System established the ITL at a moment of ferment in higher education when a host of cross-cutting challenges converged. An economic challenge emerged as revenue streams lagged behind rising costs, and a demographic challenge appeared as colleges enrolled more part-time, low-income, and nontraditional students. In addition, there was a widespread public perception that student engagement was too low, student proficiencies upon graduation too uncertain, and graduates inadequately prepared for the evolving workplace. Adding to a sense of alarm was mounting competition from for-profit universities and various online educational providers. The rise of MOOCs, the massive open online courses that attracted tens of thousands of enrollees, was especially instrumental in spurring calls for action.

It was the responsibility of the ITL, in conjunction with the system's Office of Academic Affairs, to devise a sustainable strategy to address the host of challenges facing higher education in Texas. In formulating this strategy, the ITL had to take into account lessons from the past.

HISTORICAL ANTECEDENTS

The ITL was not the first UT System–based initiative to support innovative teaching and learning. In 1998, the UT System launched the UT TeleCampus, a pioneering effort to jumpstart online learning across its campuses. At that time, UT institutions offered fewer than 10 online classes. The UT System was not alone in initiating a centralized approach to distance education. Around the same time that the UT TeleCampus was born, Pennsylvania State University opened its World Campus, and Columbia University launched its ill-fated online learning portal Fathom.

The UT TeleCampus was charged with building and delivering collaborative online courses and certificate and degree programs, and with providing a cross-institutional course registration system, a 24/7 help desk, and marketing services. At its peak, the TeleCampus offered over 30 fully online programs, with approximately 16,000 enrollments annually, and received awards for excellence from such organizations as the United States Distance Learning Association, the University Council for Educational Administration, the Texas Distance Learning Association, and the Western Interstate Commission for Higher Education (Hardy, 2011; Lederman, 2010).

In 2010, however, the UT System shuttered the TeleCampus. In retrospect, the TeleCampus was in many respects a victim of its own success. As the campuses developed their own distance education expertise, fewer were willing to participate in the development of collaborative programs, and instead rapidly developed their own online classes and degree and certificate programs. Despite its success in stimulating development of distance education across the system, the TeleCampus failed to achieve financial sustainability, and at a time of financial stringency, it seemed superfluous. Indeed, the TeleCampus was funded in part by the component campuses, which increasingly regarded those fees as a diversion of money that could be better spent on their own online programs. When the TeleCampus closed, it was delivering 250 online courses, while individual campuses were offering 2,400.

The fate of the TeleCampus offered certain significant lessons for the future. One lesson was that no centralized innovation unit would endure unless it developed a sustainable business model. Otherwise, such a unit would be unable to outlast the inevitable ups and downs of the state economy. In addition, the ITL had to acquire broad buy-in from faculty and leadership at the system's campuses and achieve a reputation for adding value to, and not for competing with, the campuses. It also had to demonstrate its capacity to foster innovations in areas that the campuses could not easily accomplish on their own. Finally, the ITL had to offer a measurable return on investment (ROI), although ROI could be defined in a variety of ways, including revenue generation, cost reductions, or discernible improvements in retention and graduation rates and time to degree.

A COLLABORATIVE APPROACH

In formulating a strategy, the ITL operated under certain constraints. Under the Texas Constitution and Regents' rules, UT System funds can only be expended on projects that are cross-institutional or that involved infrastructure serving multiple institutions. The strategy that the ITL's chief innovation officer devised balanced the power of systemness—the combined strengths of multiple institutions; the economies of scale that grow out of shared infrastructure, services, and methodology; and the breadth of impact that comes from a multicampus approach—and respect for the independence, autonomy, strengths, and individual nature of each campus (see Lane & Johnstone, 2013).

The strategy involves an "islands of innovation" approach, in which nine campuses—UT Arlington, UT Dallas, UT El Paso, UT Health Houston, UT MD Anderson, UT Permian Basin, UT Rio Grande Valley, UT San Antonio, and UT Tyler—established experimental sites where innovative future models of education could be envisaged and implemented, free from the constraints of incumbent processes, technologies, and policies.

Seven hypotheses, rooted in empirical research, guided the initiative's design. An important payoff from the initiative's data-rich approach is that it will provide the evidence necessary to test and thoroughly evaluate the design hypotheses that underlie its projects. The collection and analysis of learning data are also intended to nurture a culture of evidence across the UT System.

Hypothesis 1	Programs that offer a clear value proposition, well-defined outcomes, and pathways to mastery strengthen student motivation and persistence.

Survey research indicates that the primary reason that students give for attending college is to improve their employment opportunities, and that many students attribute their persistence in college to a direct connection between a degree and a desirable career (Covington, 2007; Fishman, 2015; Moore & Shulock, 2009; Oreopoulos & Petronijevic, 2013). In addition, research from behavioral economics reveals that motivation is enhanced when taxonomies of learning are made explicit to students, and when a program's learning objectives and the skills it imparts are explicitly linked to students' career goals (Bailey et al., 2015; Deil-Amen & Rosenbaum, 2003; Newmann et al., 2001; Ross et al., 2013).

Hypothesis 2	When learning experiences are carefully sequenced and learning pathways are optimized, student persistence increases.

Longitudinal studies indicate that student persistence improves when a program offers an optimized path to a degree, the curriculum has been intentionally designed, and the courses are synergistic (Kadlec et al., 2014). In contrast, when students' curricular options are numerous, students are prone to take courses that fail to count toward a degree (Bailey et al., 2015).

Hypothesis 3	When learning experiences are directly relevant to students' interests and professional goals, pedagogies are challenge- and performance-based and activity-driven, and learning pathways are individualized, student learning outcomes improve.

An instructional approach that encourages student engagement through active learning, that is tailored to students' learning needs and interests, and that fosters a sense of competence and a growth mindset has been shown to augment motivation, according to survey research and quantitative and qualitative studies (Allen et al., 2011; Ambrose et al., 2010; Cabrera et al., 2002; Ready, 2014; van Etten et al., 1998).

Hypothesis 4	When class schedules are predictable, students are better able to balance their studies and their work and family responsibilities and are more likely to persist in the program.

Case studies suggest that block scheduling and other delivery modalities that are adapted to students' complicated lives facilitate retention and graduation by ensuring that students can take courses at an optimal time in their curricular trajectory, allowing them to schedule their work, research, and clinical experiences more easily (Crosta, 2014).

Hypothesis 5	Rates of student success increase when support services are intensive, individualized, and readily accessible.

Access to a student success coach or an instructional facilitator who pays close attention to students' life challenges and academic needs, contacts students regularly, and provides personalized support is strongly linked to higher rates of persistence and completion (Bettinger & Baker, 2011).

Hypothesis 6	Students' metacognitive processes are strengthened when they experience frequent formative and performance-based assessments, can retake quizzes and other assessments, and have the opportunity to easily track their progress toward their educational and professional goals.

Survey research indicates that students who receive frequent formative assessment, including technology-delivered formative assessments, performed better on a variety of performance indicators than their peers, are more motivated to study, and are more aware of what they have learned and where to focus their studies (Hanover Research, 2014; Looney, 2010; Weurlander et al., 2012).

Hypothesis 7	To dramatically move the needle on student success, a program needs to simultaneously tackle student motivation, engagement, and persistence through a holistic approach to curricular design, pedagogy, learning assessment, and student support.

Case studies of highly structured programs with coherent curricula and carefully sequenced courses, shared case management systems, student tracking and early alerts, and a coaching model indicate much higher rates of retention and completion than in institutions with less structured programs (Bailey et al., 2015).

These seven hypotheses guide the design of the outcomes-focused programs. By breaking free from incumbent technologies, courses, and support structures; disaggregating courses into distinct proficiencies; creating synergist and personalized educational experiences; and emphasizing active-driven pedagogies, the UT System and its campuses seek to dramatically raise the number of students who acquire credentials in a timely fashion and better prepare the students for success in advanced education and employment.

Key elements in the UT approach include:

1. A coherent, intentionally designed curriculum consisting of synergistic courses with explicit learning outcomes, aligned with the requirements for success in high-demand career fields

2. The division of courses into highly focused, granular units of instruction, with clearly defined learning goals and tightly aligned assessments, creating multiple entry points for students, depending on their prior knowledge and the ability to personalize learning trajectories

3. A commitment to high-impact pedagogies and active learning through advanced simulations; problem-solving; and project-, case-, and team-based learning, as well as to multiple levels of assessment, including checks for understanding, practice sets, and problem-solving exercises and project- and team-based assessments

4. Gamification of the learning experience to increase engagement and motivation by allowing students to acquire points as they complete activities, receive micro-certifications, and advance from one level of attainment to the next

5. Schedules and delivery modes that make it easier for students to balance their studies and their familial and workplace responsibilities

6. A next-generation digital learning platform capable of delivering multimedia content, facilitating collaboration,

and integrating data from multiple silos and providing actionable insights into student engagement, persistence, and performance, as well as measures of self-efficacy

7. A "community of care" to cultivate student success skills, ensure that students are making steady progress toward achieving their goals, and provide timely assistance when needed

8. An emphasis on research to inform continuous improvement of the learning experience and contribute to the learning sciences

HOW IT HAPPENED

The first step in our design and development process was to conduct extensive market research to identify fields that combined high employer and student demand. These fields included the health professions, engineering, computer science, criminal justice, and business. A request for proposals (RFP) was issued to the campuses inviting departments and colleges to propose innovative programs in those high-demand fields. Twenty-two proposals were submitted for consideration, and 10 were selected through a rigorous review process. Memorandums of understanding (MOUs) were subsequently signed, specifying roles, policies, timetables, and targeted benchmarks. The portfolio includes an early prototype initiative, a bachelor of science program in biomedical sciences that launched in August 2015 at UT Rio Grande Valley. Second-phase prototypes in nursing, cybersecurity, industrial engineering, electrical engineering, and energy technology management enrolled students in fall 2017.

In return for funding of up to $6 million per program to ensure a high-quality learning experience, the participating departments and colleges agreed to work closely with the ITL staff and select teams of instructional design, production, and student lifecycle management professionals through the design and implementation phases of each project. They also agreed that programs would be operated on a common platform (Total Educational Experience, or TEx), and that all content assets (including learning objects, case- and team-based learning scaffolds, assessments, and media) produced through this initiative would be made available to faculty across the system for use in a wide range of programming use cases. In addition to receiving design, technical, and operational support from the ITL and select vendor partners, the grantees receive:

- Membership in a systemwide design and research consortium, which will serve as a solver community for working through critical path opportunities and challenges related to the design and deployment of outcomes-oriented pathways, and contribute to the national visibility of the initiative

- Designation as a UT System x-site, an experimental site that will serve as a model for innovation in curricular design, program delivery, pedagogy, and educational research

- Holistic student support through TEx, the technology, service, and analytics platform

- Research to study and validate program outcomes and impacts

At each experimental site, cross-disciplinary teams of faculty—in conjunction with curriculum and instructional designers, learning architects, educational technologists, accreditation experts, and assessment specialists, as well as with input from professional associations, standard-setting organizations, and industry advisories—define the audience and design requirements for the program. The guiding coalition constructs a knowledge grid or scaffold that disaggregates existing degree pathways into discrete concepts, skills, and measurable learning outcomes. These graphs are complex and dynamic, sketching out hundreds of outcomes across multiple levels of competency. This grid serves as the program's master blueprint and can support multiple pathways, including stand-alone modules, micro-certificates, stackable credentials, and degrees. At the same time, campus faculty members and student and academic affairs leaders plan all aspects of the new pathways from the optimal delivery modality (face-to-face, hybrid, or online), to academic operations and supporting technologies and services.

Once an outcomes grid is articulated, faculty, instructional designers, and assessment experts develop extremely granular—"atomic"—units of instruction. This atomic approach to design allows the design team to efficiently update students' learning experiences as specific impacts on student behavior and performance are revealed. Equally important, this approach allows us to create personalized learning pathways tailored to each learner's strengths, challenges, prior experiences, and aspirations. Our programming models give credit to prior learning and to formal and informal professional experiences. Robust preadmissions coaching guides students as they set pathway and completion goals according to their unique incoming profiles. Once enrolled in any given program of study, students are encouraged to set reasonable pace targets and make instructional content choices (including access to bilingual content) to address their academic strengths and challenges.

After blueprinting is completed, the development phase begins. The production team analyzes existing content and learning objects and outlines additional materials needed to support high-impact pedagogies, including instructional videos, graphics, practice sets, assessments, cases, simulations, learning objects, and discussion activities. Then, the faculty design team approves the module blueprints and related project timelines, and the instructional design coordinator develops a content curation and production project planner based on the knowledge and skills map for each module. The production team, employing relevant subject matter expertise, curates content against the knowledge map, starting with open educational resources, and then, as necessary, moving into licensable published materials and learning objects. Using this baseline content, the production team and instructional design coordinators develop learning arcs using rapid prototyping and iterative design. With each iteration, the faculty design team reviews sample learning activities and assessments. Based on feedback, the production team and instructional design coordinators revise and inform the next round of content curation and learning arc production.

Once all course content, activities, and assessments have been uploaded into the system, the production team inserts all visual design treatments and graphical elements to ensure that the experience has a beautiful look and an engaging feel. To wrap up the course build, the instructional design coordinators oversee the authentication of all course elements. The faculty design team then reviews the course and signs off on the program's readiness to "go live."

Meanwhile, ITL staff work closely with campus faculty members and student and academic affairs leaders to plan all aspects of program delivery to drive much higher rates of student retention, completion, and post-program success. This guiding coalition determines the most optimal delivery modality, whether this is face-to-face, hybrid, or fully online; it also establishes program policies and organizes student support services and program operations.

Supporting all programming pathways is our next-generation digital learning platform, TEx. This mobile-first platform provides an elegant, consistent user experience as students move from module to certificate to degree and beyond. Unlike a traditional learning management system, which assumes that students move through the curriculum in a linear fashion at a standardized pace and according to a fixed calendar, TEx supports individualized learning pathways and variable pace. The vehicle through which students interact with digital laboratories and simulations, participate in collaborative activities, explore transmedia case materials, and take part in peer critiques, TEx also delivers rich multimedia content as well as highly interactive and connected learning experiences.

Equally important, TEx is capable of integrating data from multiple data silos, including the Student Information System, the Learning Management System, content services, and an array of learning and assessment applications. By offering near real-time insights into student pace, engagement, persistence, and performance, TEx empowers faculty and staff to provide high-touch services to those students most in need of encouragement and to tailor support to individual student needs. TEx's data collection capabilities also promote empirical research into student learning and continuous improvement of program and curriculum design, pedagogy, and student services operations.

The personalized online component of the curriculum delivered through TEx serves as the spinal column for each learner's experience. TEx presents curated content (the same kinds of content students currently obtain from costly textbooks—except more interactive, more up-to-date, and from a greater diversity of trustworthy sources) through an activity-driven approach. As learners move through each set of what are, essentially, dynamically designed homework exercises, the system continuously diagnoses their strengths and challenges and serves up high-fidelity content that aligns with personal preferences. TEx automatically accelerates or decelerates the pace of students as they work through their studies, encouraging learners to spend their time more efficiently and with greater impact on their development. Students who fall behind critical pace markers receive just-in-time interventions from faculty or instructional facilitators to keep them on track.

To better support students at every stage of the student lifecycle and increase rates of student satisfaction, retention, graduation, and postgraduation success, our outcomes-oriented programs offer redesigned student lifecycle management and constituent relationship systems to improve communication, enhance student support, and provide access to data that can improve instruction, prompt timely interventions, and continuously improve the educational experience.

This next generation approach is built around a progressive student profile (PSP), which provides a comprehensive record of students' academic and professional goals, prior learning experiences, and emergent competencies—and how these characteristics are aligned with the job market. By consolidating information from multiple data silos, our data infrastructure allows faculty and advisors to acquire a holistic and integrated perspective on each student's strengths and needs and the information required to serve students optimally. Learning dashboards help students, faculty members, and advisors monitor students' progress toward a degree and alert them in near real time when students are off course to enable more timely interventions.

LESSONS LEARNED

Rigorous assessment is integral to the success of this project. Stakeholders at all levels need to know whether a holistic, competency-based, outcomes-focused approach to curriculum design, pedagogy, instructional staffing, and student support can make a substantial difference in student learning outcomes, and whether such an approach is replicable, scalable, and financially sustainable. With its progressive personal student profile and its ability to ingest high-quality data about student engagement and learning from multiple silos, the project is designed to facilitate a thorough assessment.

For outcomes-oriented programs, valid, reliable, and accurate assessment is of critical importance. It is needed to validate student learning, assess outcomes, and drive continuous improvement of the learning experience that the programs offer. In the first of the programs to go live, the bachelor of science in biomedical sciences at UT Rio Grande Valley, the faculty design team worked with the Council for Aid to Education, the creator of the Collegiate Learning Assessment, to design assessments to ensure the accuracy and validity of student learning assessments and their alignment with the program's learning objectives and with proficiencies defined by professional associations and industry.

The UT System is equally interested in program- and project-level assessment. Only in this way can we determine whether our interventions make a measurable and significant difference in student outcomes. Drawing in part upon detailed evidence collected by the data infrastructure, the ITL's data science team and other researchers will measure the number of students who experience the revised curriculum, evaluate how their learning outcomes and engagement compare to students in existing programs, and assess whether the new pathways produce higher levels of student retention and completion. In addition, the evaluators will assess the design process and analyze correlations between program features, students' interactions with the TEx system, and academic outcomes.

The approach that the UT System is taking toward innovation is anything but business as usual. Curricula are designed collaboratively by teams that include input from professional associations, industry, and content experts across and outside the UT System. The design team works in partnership with best-in-breed innovators in areas of instructional design, user experience development, educational technology, content curation, and assessment. The learning experience, in turn, is designed to monitor student engagement and learning. Students are provided with life coaches and instructional facilitators to provide the support and point of contact that many need if they are to succeed. Meanwhile, all costs are clearly defined, so that administrators know the precise price of each program element.

Such an approach is expensive. But if the system and campuses are to create scalable, replicable models that significantly boost student persistence and graduation rates, the ROI will greatly outweigh the costs, while freeing faculty to devote more time to the high-impact practices—including guided research, intensive mentoring, and supervised experiential learning—that will greatly enhance the student experience.

CHAPTER 6 TAKEAWAYS

- Systems are ideally situated to support advancement of new learning modalities, particularly those supported by new technologies.

- System-level innovation efforts need to develop sustainable business models to withstand economic tumults and campus competition.

- Campuses were allowed to create "islands of innovation" or zones where new learning models can be developed without constraints of existing policies, practices, and technologies.

- Innovation needs to be sustained and enhanced through a model of continuous improvement.

- Collaboration across professional associations, employers, and content experts is combined with expertise in instructional design, user experience, and assessment to create a new learning experience.

REFERENCES

Allen, D. E., Donham, R. S., & Bernhardt, S. A. (2011). Problem based learning. *New Directions for Teaching and Learning,* 21–29. doi:10.1002/tl.465

Ambrose, S. A., Bridges, M. W., DiPietro, M., Lovett, M. C., & Norman, M. K. (2010). *How learning works: Seven research-based principles for smart teaching.* Wiley.

Bailey, T. R., Jaggars, S. S., & Jenkins, D. (2015). *Redesigning America's community colleges: A clearer path to student success.* Harvard University Press.

Bettinger, E., & Baker, R. (2011). *The effects of student coaching in college: An evaluation of a randomized experiment in student mentoring* (NBER Working Paper No. 16881). National Bureau of Economic Research. http://www.nber.org/papers/w16881

Cabrera, A. F., Crissman, J. L., Bernal, E. M., Nora, A., Terenzini, P. T., & Pascarella, E. T. (2002). Collaborative learning: Its impact on college students' development and diversity. *Journal of College Student Development, 43*(1), 20–34.

Covington, M. V. (2007). A motivational analysis of academic life in college. In R. P. Perry & J. C. Smart (Eds.), *The scholarship of teaching and learning in higher education: An evidence-based perspective* (pp. 661–729). Springer.

Crosta, P. M. (2014). Intensity and attachment: How the chaotic enrollment patterns of community college students relate to educational outcomes. *Community College Review, 42,* 118–142. doi:10.1177/0091552113518233

Deil-Amen, R. J., & Rosenbaum, J. E. (2003). The social prerequisites of success: Can college structure reduce the need for social know-how? *Annals of the American Academy of Political and Social Science, 586,* 120–143. doi:10.1177/0002716202250216

Fishman, R. (2015). *2015 college decision survey: Part I—Deciding to go to college.* New America Foundation EdCentral. http://www.edcentral.org/wp-content/uploads/2015/05/FINAL-College-Decisions-Survey-528.pdf

Hanover Research. (2014). *The impact of formative assessment and learning intentions on student achievement.* http://www.

hanoverresearch.com/media/The-Impact-of-Formative-Assessment-and-Learning-Intentions-on-Student-Achievement.pdf

Hardy, D. W. (2011). Before the fall: Breaking rules and changing minds. In E. J. Burge, C. C. Gibson & T. Gibson (Eds.), *Flexible pedagogy, flexible practice: Notes from the trenches of distance education* (pp. 111–126). AU Press.

Kadlec, A., Immerwahr, J., & Gupta, J. (2014). *Guided pathways to student success: Perspectives from Indiana college students & advisors.* Indiana Commission for Higher Education. http://www.in.gov/che/files/3-FINAL-PA-ICHE_Guided_Pathways_Research_9_10_2013.pdf

Lane, J. E., & Johnstone, D. B. (eds.). (2013). *Higher education systems 3.0: Harnessing systemness, delivering performance.* State University of New York Press.

Lederman, D. (2010, April 9). Texas kills its TeleCampus. *Inside Higher Ed.* https://www.insidehighered.com/news/2010/04/09/TeleCampus

Looney, J. (2010). *Making it happen: Formative assessment and educational technologies* (Thinking Deeper Research Paper No. 1, Part 3). Promethean Education Strategy Group. http://www.innovationunit.org/sites/default/files/Promethean%20-%20Thinking%20Deeper%20Research%20Paper%20part%203.pdf

Moore, C., & Shulock, N. (2009). *Student progress toward degree completion: Lessons from the research literature.* Institute for Higher Education Leadership & Policy.

Newmann, F. M., Smith, B., Allensworth, E., & Bryk, A. S. (2001). Instructional program coherence: What it is and why it should guide school improvement policy. *Educational Evaluation and Policy Analysis, 23,* 297–321. doi:10.3102/01623737023004297

Oreopoulos, P., & Petronijevic, U. (2013). *Making college worth it: A review of research on the returns to higher education* (NBER Working Paper No. 19053). National Bureau of Economic Research. http://www.nber.org/papers/w19053.pdf

Ready, D. D. (2014). *Student mathematics performance in the first two years of Teach to One: Math.* New Classrooms. http://www.newclassrooms.org/resources/Teach-to-One_Report_2013-14.pdf

Ross, R., White, S., Wright, J., & Knapp, L. (2013). *Using behavioral economics for postsecondary success*. Citi Foundation. http://www.citifoundation.com/citi/foundation/pdf/ideas42.pdf

van Etten, S., Pressley, M., Freebern, G., & Echevarria, M. (1998). An interview study of college freshmens' beliefs about their academic motivation. *European Journal of Psychology of Education, 13*, 105–130. doi:10.1007/BF03172816

Weurlander, M., Söderberg, M., Scheja, M., Hult, H., & Wernerson, A. (2012). Exploring formative assessment as a tool for learning: Students' experiences of different methods of formative assessment. *Assessment & Evaluation in Higher Education, 37*, 747–760. doi:10.1080/02602938.2011.572153

7

ENABLING A CULTURE OF ACADEMIC INNOVATION

Lessons Learned from a Systemwide Course Redesign Initiative

JOANN A. BOUGHMAN AND M. J. BISHOP

ABSTRACT

Public higher education systems are under pressure to transform in ways that might meaningfully and sustainably improve the educational achievement of their students. But, to date, higher education has a weak history of academic innovations that have led to these kinds of transformations. This is not due to some extraordinary resistance to change, but rather to the complexities inherent in the academic institutional culture that keep higher education from fitting neatly into traditional innovation adoption models. Recently, we took time to reflect on the University System of Maryland's successful eight-year, systemwide course redesign initiative in order to evaluate the *System's* role in enabling academic innovation to generate transformational change. Using complex adaptive systems theory as a framework for analysis, this chapter reports the findings of that qualitative self-study of the system's role in leading academic change—specifically, the extent to which USM was able to cultivate a culture of innovation across its member institutions.

Joann A. Boughman and M. J. Bishop led this work in their roles with the University System of Maryland.

All of public higher education, campuses and systems, are facing the same challenge: how to improve the educational achievement of their students meaningfully and sustainably, especially those from underserved minorities and lower income distributions who have far lower prospects for graduation and degree attainment (Korn, 2015). At the same time, education leaders can also expect ongoing public-sector resource shortages, which translate into reductions in higher education appropriations and make problems of student success even more challenging (Geiger, 2010). State systems may be uniquely positioned to address these challenges—more so than individual postsecondary institutions—by sharing resources and best practices, collaborating on degree programs, working with employers to tailor offerings to their state's workforce needs, driving greater effectiveness and efficiency, and promoting policy and business models to incentivize innovations focused on student success and transforming higher education (Zimpher, 2013).

Eckel and colleagues (1998) defined *transformational change* as that which "1) alters the culture of the institution by changing select underlying assumptions and institutional behaviors, processes, and products; 2) is deep and pervasive, affecting the whole institution; 3) is intentional; and 4) occurs over time" (p. 3). To date, however, higher education has a weak history of academic innovations that have led to these kinds of transformations. We submit that this situation is not the consequence of some extraordinary resistance to change by educators or to a fundamental lack of trying across academe, but rather that there are complexities inherent in the academic institutional culture that keep higher education from fitting neatly into traditional innovation adoption models. It appears that bringing academic innovations to scale for transformational change may be as much about understanding and addressing the complex institutional culture as it is about adopting emerging technologies and incorporating evidence-based practice (Kezar & Eckel, 2002a, 2002b). Stated differently, overcoming the myriad structural, organizational, and attitudinal barriers to achieving meaningful and lasting change from innovations in higher education is a cultural process, necessitating a more nuanced approach than simply getting sheer numbers of faculty, staff, and students to participate in an initiative. The change must come from full engagement of institutional staff and faculty focused on learning outcomes beyond course grades on a transcript. This transformation will require new communication strategies across *silos* and more effective messaging from leadership.

As part of its commitment to improving student success, in 2006 the University System of Maryland (USM) began what became a series of initiatives aimed at redesigning courses across its campuses to make them more learning centered, with a focus on large-enrollment, lower-division, gateway courses with unacceptably high "D" grade, failure, and withdrawal (DFW) rates. The goal for most of these redesigns was to maintain or improve learning outcomes and reduce "course drift" (variation of content and standards across sections) while also freeing up faculty resources. Rather than spending the majority of class time lecturing, faculty used class time to engage students directly in a variety of activities and offloaded "content delivery" to other vehicles (e.g., readings, videotaped lectures). Fifty-seven courses were ultimately redesigned, incorporating many new learning-centered practices such as group work and computer tutorials in class, online homework with rapid feedback, and coaching by undergraduate learning assistants. The USM's course redesign initiatives achieved considerable success, lowering DFW rates by an average of 7 percent while freeing up over $5.5 million in faculty resources for reallocation. More importantly, more than 143,000 students were impacted, and a cumulative 10,200 students passed who might not have—had the courses not been redesigned.

But what role did the *System* play in leading this academic change, and how well did it do?

Using support from the Bill & Melinda Gates Foundation, we reflected on the USM's eight-year, systemwide course redesign initiative to evaluate the System's role in enabling this academic innovation to generate transformational change. The goal of this research was to determine opportunities for, and limits on, actions undertaken by higher education system administrations in support of academic change; to describe how circumstances combined to make it difficult to scale an innovation like course redesign; and to outline a strategy that, over time, may have a better chance of creating transformational change from system-led initiatives in the future.

From September 2014 through May 2015, over 70 individuals—from the USM chancellor to faculty and students—from across the

System were interviewed or participated in focus groups, many of them several times. Each of the 11 USM institutions that participated in course redesign was visited at least once. Planning documents and final reports of each redesign were studied, and the leaders of the redesigned courses were surveyed. The collected data were analyzed to pinpoint, examine, and identify patterns and themes. Initial drafts of the findings and emerging themes from those data were vetted by various stakeholders to assure that our interpretations represented participants' voices accurately. The final report to the Gates Foundation, *Improving Graduation Outcomes by Spreading and Sustaining Learning-Centered Practices* (Ehrmann & Bishop, 2015), summarize our findings in creating the institutional conditions necessary to encourage faculty involvement in course redesign activities and assuring those innovations are sufficiently substantive and sustainable to improve student success. The current chapter focuses more broadly on the System's role in leading academic change—specifically, the extent to which the USM was able to cultivate a culture of innovation across its member institutions. Reflecting on the organic and evolutionary development of these changes has provided insights and opportunities to capitalize on our initial successes and refocus our activities on areas where gaps were identified.

BACKGROUND: THE USM AND COURSE REDESIGN

The USM is best described as a "comprehensive system" in that it represents much of the institutional diversity of US four-year public education as well as the great population diversity within the state of Maryland (Lane, 2013). The USM was formed in 1988 with the merger of the five University of Maryland institutions and the six members of the State University and College System of Maryland. While the University of Maryland College Park enjoys the status and support as the flagship campus, the USM functions as a federation of institutions, each having a unique mission focused on the various strengths required to meet the needs of the state's diverse student population. Therefore, the USM's 14 campuses include three research-intensive schools (including a professional schools campus), four comprehensive institutions located in a mix of urban and rural settings, three historically Black institutions, one distance-learning university, a degree-conferring center for environmental science, and two regional centers.[1] System-level policies provide the framework for institutional policies and procedures, and reports curated by the USM office are provided both to our single governing Board of Regents and the Maryland Higher Education Commission.

The USM is at a great advantage compared to many state systems because of Maryland's relatively small geographic footprint; inter-institutional groups can meet frequently in face-to-face gatherings that permit open exchange of ideas, sharing of best practices, and the development of familiarity and trust among colleagues. A Council of University System Presidents, an Academic Affairs Advisory Council (provosts), the vice presidents for student affairs, the CIOs, and vice presidents for administration and finance all meet on a monthly basis to exchange information, share ideas, and give the USM an opportunity to facilitate collaborations among the campuses. In addition, the USM convenes workgroups of experts representing different constituencies to focus on specific policy developments or inter-institutional initiatives.

Effectiveness and efficiency. Responding to economic challenges, in 2004 the USM Board of Regents launched an effectiveness and efficiency (E&E) initiative to make better use of available resources. E&E began by discovering ways to save on administrative processes, but by 2005, discussions were underway about achieving greater effectiveness and efficiency in academic processes as well. In early 2006, the Board of Regents called on Chancellor William E. ("Brit") Kirwan to organize a Maryland Course Redesign Initiative (MCRI) based on the work being done by the National Center on Academic Transformation (NCAT). NCAT's vision of course redesign involved making changes to improve both quality and "cost-saving," which was NCAT's label for reducing the amount of time faculty members dedicated to a course, thereby freeing them to engage in other activities. NCAT's course redesign process targeted large enrollment, multisection courses that often have unacceptably high DFW rates.

The Board of Regents expected action, so the USM quickly allocated about $500,000 of one-time money to the MCRI, which supplied matching grants to system institutions and covered NCAT consulting help over the three years of this initial course redesign project. Each institution's provost was invited to nominate a single course for redesign, and System staff visited many USM campuses to explain the process. The solicitation sent from the System Office to USM's degree-granting institutions explained that the goals of the program were to simultaneously

- Adopt new ways to improve student learning outcomes
- Demonstrate these improvements through rigorous assessment
- Reduce institutional costs
- Free up instructional resources for other purposes
- Develop the internal capacity of USM faculty and staff to continue the redesign process

All but one of the System campuses ultimately submitted a course to redesign as part of the project. Course redesign began later in 2007 and continued through 2014 with subsequent support from a Carnegie Mellon award, a USM fundraising campaign in honor of Chancellor Kirwan, and grants from the Lumina Foundation and Complete College America.

USM course redesign project procedures. The System provided grants of $20,000 per redesigned course to institutions that were willing to commit to matching $20,000 (for a total of $40,000 per project). While most of the funds went to compensate faculty time, some projects used resources to renovate classrooms to support student use of technology.

Most of the courses targeted for redesign were multisection classes involving multiple instructors. In most cases, therefore, teams of faculty members worked together to develop a new design and then try it on just one section of their multisection course. From this trial they collected DFW rates, student outcomes (such as scores on a common final exam), and teaching experiences in the redesigned version of the course and compared those data to traditional sections of the same course. The next step, often taking a year to complete, was to tweak the design based on findings from the pilot, then fully implement the new design across all sections of the course.

To support the faculty's work, USM leaders of the initiative organized a series of workshops intended to (a) teach faculty the basics of redesign; (b) create a setting to share ideas and experiences at the midway point of the project; and (c) provide a final, capstone opportunity to share their findings after the courses were fully implemented and summatively assessed. The early results from the redesigns were good, with reduced DFW rates, usually improved or similar learning outcomes, and faculty time freed for other purposes.

During the second half of the initiative under Carnegie funding, the USM named six course redesign faculty fellows, all of whom had distinguished themselves as leaders of the initial MCRI redesigns. The fellows reviewed proposals for redesigns, developed and led workshops for the incoming faculty redesigners, worked to foster more redesign activity in their home institutions, and provided one-on-one coaching and peer support for colleagues from other institutions in their disciplinary areas. The fellows also shared experiences and insights with faculty designers about programmatic strategies. Due to their work writing articles, making conference presentations, and running workshops, the fellows became the face of the redesign initiative in many ways—not just within the USM, but also outside the System.

IMPACT OF THE USM'S COURSE REDESIGN INITIATIVES

As discussed earlier, the direct impact of the USM's course redesign initiatives were clear: a cumulative 7 percent drop in DFW rates with $5.5 million in instructional cost savings for reallocation. Indirectly, the initiatives resulted in other advances as well, at both the system and institutional levels.

Impacts at the system level. Influenced by the success of MCRI, the Carnegie gift, and the Lumina grant, the USM's 2010 strategic plan (USM Board of Regents, 2010) made academic transformation a major priority. To help implement the strategic plan, Chancellor Kirwan and the Board of Regents made academic transformation an annual performance goal for all USM institutional presidents. Academic transformation also became a standing agenda item for the monthly meeting of USM provosts and was frequently a topic on the agenda of other systemwide meetings of senior officials, such as the CIOs and the vice presidents for student affairs.

For the first few years, academic transformation was almost synonymous with "course redesign" within the USM, but use of academic transformation eventually broadened to include a variety of innovations underway across USM campuses aimed at improving student success by making higher education more accessible, affordable, and effective. By 2010 the System had published a new 10-year strategic plan that identified, as one of its five themes, "transforming the academic model." The plan asserted:

> Many elements of the academic model under which we have been operating for the last century are becoming unsustainable financially, outdated pedagogically, and obsolete technologically. Not least among these forces is growing public demand that our institutions be more forthright and accountable for what they expect graduates to learn and be prepared to do. (USM Board of Regents, 2010, p. 17)

The plan called for USM institutions to develop a comprehensive process for exploring academic innovations, expanding current change efforts, and creating a formal structure to support and sustain transformational ideas as they emerged. The establishment and specification of clearly articulated goals helped to reduce complexity and create a context for academic innovation.

All this activity helped make the case that more state funding was needed to support USM academic transformation initiatives. For FY2014, the System received enhancement funding from the Maryland General Assembly that, in combination with institutional matching, allocated $5.8 million more to academic transformation across USM institutions. In 2013 the USM Board of Regents approved the creation of a system-level center, now named the William E. Kirwan Center for Academic Innovation, to provide a resource for facilitating academic innovation and transformative change across the System. Funds were allocated to the Center from the enhancement funds in FY2014.

Impacts at the institutional level. Starting with the campus matches for course redesign, System leaders hoped that campuses would encourage and fully finance ongoing and expanded innovations that would be financed wholly with institutional funds. Faculty fellows also encouraged colleagues to become involved.

Course redesign has continued through campus-led initiatives using state enhancement funds as well as other support, but while the campuses continued to view redesign work as important after USM support ended, the institutionalization of the initiative was rather limited and uneven. Instead, the most striking impact of the course redesign initiative is the extent to which it helped ignite other academic change efforts, including the development of fully online programs; the exploration of MOOCs; the use of learning analytics; and the adoption of open educational resources, competency-based approaches, and—most recently—adaptive learning tools. To support these initiatives, many USM institutions have created new positions to coordinate their work on academic change campus-wide.

Seven USM campuses—including the two regional centers—now have full-time academic innovation leadership positions in the provost's office/academic affairs. The other seven universities have appointed academic innovation leaders who, as a dedicated part of their duties, work regularly with their provost's office on these initiatives. The Kirwan Center regularly convenes this group of academic change leaders—now named the Academic Transformation Advisory Council (ATAC)—to work on strategic initiatives as well as policy questions for the System and the legislature. ATAC members bring a vast knowledge and understanding of the challenges facing their campuses and of the innovative work within their institutions. Council members serve a critical role as liaisons and advocates for their institutions and the center. ATAC meets at least six times per year to generate ideas, find ways to collaborate, help shape the Kirwan Center's agenda, advance innovative programs and projects, and disseminate information back to the institutions. The Kirwan Center has also organized a systemwide Council for Program and Faculty Development (CPFD), which brings together leaders of teaching centers and faculty development programs to help each other more effectively foster teaching improvement in their institutions while working within the constraints of increasingly limited budgets and staff.

The USM's investment in course redesign has done more than establish model courses on each campus. By tapping into faculty and administrative leaders and promoting ongoing conversations around academic transformation, the USM succeeded in building systemwide capacity for academic innovation, which led to the establishment of the Kirwan Center and the development of an infrastructure to support change on the campuses. We now have an engaged academic community eager to explore innovative new models for improving student success. Moving forward, it will be important to find ways for the System to sustain this innovation culture toward achieving transformative change.

But making sense of whether the many variables of the USM's course redesign initiative interacted to create these outcomes is a difficult task. Dynamic social systems such as education have far too many interacting variables to be reduced easily to a set of linear, cause-and-effect relationships (Banathy, 1991). Instead, it appears that understanding the ways in which the USM might have enabled this culture of academic innovation requires a systems approach to inquiry.

A COMPLEX ADAPTIVE SYSTEMS FRAMEWORK FOR ANALYSIS

A *system*[2] is a group of parts or elements that work as a functional whole when coupled together (Hall & Fagen, 1956). In 1995, Holland noted that there are some kinds of systems that can be fairly easily modeled and simulated—such as the flow of air over an airplane wing. He observed that there are, however, "systems of crucial interest to humankind that have so far defied accurate simulation by computer," including economies, ecologies, immune systems, and the brain (Holland, 1995, p. 17). These *complex adaptive systems* all have a similar "evolving structure" in that they "change and reorganize their component parts to adapt themselves to the problems posed by their surroundings"—consequently making them very difficult to study and control as well (Holland, 1995, p. 18). Nonetheless, with the advent of analytic technologies that allow new ways of storing, organizing, displaying, and interacting with huge data sets, scholars have begun validating Holland's 20-year-old hypothesis that mechanisms mediating systems are much more alike than surface observations would suggest (Holland, 1995, p. 18).

Researchers using these sophisticated new analytics technologies, such as Uhl-Bien and colleagues (2007), have characterized complex adaptive systems as "neural-like networks of interacting, interdependent agents who are bonded in a cooperative dynamic by a common goal, outlook, need, etc." (p. 299). In complex adaptive systems, "agents, events, and ideas bump into each other in somewhat unpredictable fashion, and change emerges from this dynamic interactive process" (Uhl-Bien et al., 2007, p. 302). Similarly, Keshavarz and associates (2010) identified the key characteristics of complex adaptive systems, which they have observed

- Learn and adapt in continually changing ways depending on the context

- Retain distributed network control rather than centralized hierarchical control

- Are "nested"

- Exhibit "emergence" (the interplay of agents shape a hidden but recognizable regularity in the behavior of the whole system)

Based on the findings from their research on education systems, Keshavarz et al. (2010) emphasized the unique characteristics of *social* complex adaptive systems. These systems are more multifaceted as they introduce additional properties such as human nature, social norms, and variation (two parallel subsystems operating with competing rules, values, and interaction patterns). While human agents in social complex adaptive systems are free to choose when and how to interact, over time some interactions begin to occur more frequently due to the influence of system *attractors*[3] that create clear boundaries for behavior (Hirsch et al., 2004). As systemwide patterns of behavior emerge, they reinforce others' behaviors, which subsequently strengthen the patterns. These emergent patterns make up the *culture* of a social complex adaptive system (Eoyang & Holladay, 2013).

The characteristics of social complex adaptive systems can make it difficult to know how a higher education system will react to change—much less to know how to lead change within it. In fact, complexity scholars have argued that existing leadership theory is not particularly well suited to address the intricacies of these rapidly changing environments because traditional models are often premised on a particular individual's efforts to create stability and eliminate uncertainty through organizational structure and hierarchy (see Child & McGrath, 2001; Ilinitch et al., 1996; Levin & Fullan, 2008). Uhl-Bien and associates (2007) argued that leadership in complex adaptive systems

> should not be seen only as position and authority but also as an *emergent, interactive dynamic*—a complex interplay from which a collective impetus for action and change emerges when heterogeneous agents interact in networks in ways that produce new patterns of behavior or new modes of operating. (p. 299)

Hazy (2011) further suggested that understanding complex adaptive systems—and transformational leadership within them—requires a shift from thinking about system structures to focusing analyses on *interrelations* within the system instead. In this context, leadership is viewed not as a top-down function of corporate decision-making; rather, leadership is just one of several "organizational capabilities that directly relate to an organization's performance and adaptability" (Hazy, 2011, p. 168).

Hazy (2011) identified three leadership capacities within complex adaptive systems: generative, unifying, and convergent.[4] *Generative leadership* is adaptive—learning and creating innovative responses to changes in the environment. At the other extreme, *convergent leadership* serves an orienting and coordinating structure—working to achieve outcomes preestablished by the institution in as effective a manner as possible. *Unifying leadership* works between these two ends of the spectrum—creating balance between the emergent and bureaucratic functions of the system while also managing the inevitable "entanglements" between them. According to Uhl-Bien et al. (2007), striking this unifying balance means creating the conditions that allow generative leadership to thrive where innovation is needed while also "facilitating the flow of knowledge and creativity from adaptive structures into administrative structures" (p. 305).

In 2011, Hazy depicted these interrelationships among the three leadership capacities within a complex adaptive system and how they exploit existing capabilities and/or explore new capabilities to adapt to the changing environment (see figure 7.1). As illustrated, *convergent leadership* works to exploit existing resources by improving the quality of current programs and reducing transaction costs—to increase efficiency within the system. This activity is aimed at making incremental improvements by testing specific changes to existing capabilities, evaluating the result, and either retaining or abandoning the change. As efficiencies are gained, surplus resources become available for use in new programs and, eventually, the system approaches a level of "peak performance." It is important that convergent leadership avoid complacency—a situation where the system's performance is deemed to be "good enough" despite the fact that continual changes in the environment

Figure 7.1. Hazy's Leadership and Capabilities Model (LCM)

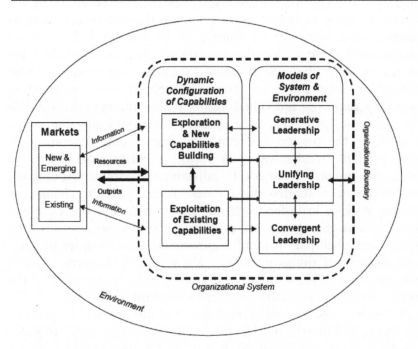

make it increasingly likely the structure has become ineffective and needs to be recalibrated.

Hazy (2011) suggested that to ensure sustainability over time by creating variety in the system, *generative leadership* must use the surplus resources saved through convergent leadership activities to explore the environment and the system's structure for new opportunities. Generative leadership promotes iterative prototyping and testing of innovations to accumulate knowledge both about the opportunity itself as well as its feasibility within the system's context. While this process consumes stored resources with little or no guarantee there will ever be any benefit, changes in the environment make continual exploration and experimentation with "constructive deviations" from common practice necessary for the system's survival. In this sense, generative leadership is not a single person but rather the result of many enacted events that focus collective attention and align information gathering and exploration activities in the system to capitalize on opportunities (Hazy, 2011, p. 181).

According to Hazy (2011), the obvious tensions arising between generative and convergent leadership can be released either by the system changing its boundaries to contain the differences (such as spinning off a new unit or venture) or by reshaping the system's culture—and even its identity—to absorb and accommodate the differences (such changing its values, purpose, and mission). These cultural changes can reverberate throughout the organization, eventually requiring individual agents within the system to decide whether to accept or reject the changes. *Unifying leadership* works to alleviate the tension between convergence and generation by using available mechanisms and adjusting existing parameters to change the system's dynamics. By adjusting the parameters, unifying leadership can create new possibilities for the system to change (by relaxing policies in order to permit experimentation, for example) or to refocus the system on existing pathways (such as creating tightly prescribed parameters for experimentation in order to minimize damages if things go awry). Hazy (2011) observed, "These dynamics lead to the formation, distortion, and reformation of the organization into alternate organizational forms" (p. 184).

Combined, the leadership regulates all of this activity "by generating, using, and improving the system and the environment to guide decision and action" (Hazy, 2011, p. 174). Creative problem-solving is achieved organically in complex adaptive systems through the work of structured social networks rather than by centralized authorities (Uhl-Bien et al., 2007). Catalyzing this activity requires increasing the information flow and interaction rates among these social networks that, in turn, generate new ideas and possibilities for the overall system as it responds to changes in the environment (Ashby, 1962; Reschke et al., 2010). Hazy and Uhl-Bien (2014) suggested that, in this way, complex systems leadership is really more of a *social process* that changes the rules of interaction within the system, primarily through indirect mechanisms and consistent and constant communication (see also Mumford & Licuanan, 2004; Surie & Hazy, 2006).

As a result of the myriad interactions among agents, complexity science has found that persistent emergent patterns of system-level changes begin to emerge in the organization. Complexity science studies the dynamic structures and properties of these qualitatively different "states of being" and seeks to explain the mechanisms necessary for them to emerge (Hazy, 2012; Hazy et al., 2011; Hazy et al., 2010).

APPLYING THE FRAMEWORK

Given that leadership in complex adaptive systems self-organizes out of the interactions of its agents, it would be easy to assume there is no role for system-level leadership. However, complexity theorists like Surie and Hazy (2006) have argued that "it is not simply the composition of the team or the ability to increase interactions but *how* interactions are managed and regulated that leads to innovation" (p. 15). The trick is to find ways to establish new system attractors that will change the system's patterns of behavior—and eventually its culture.

Applying complex adaptive systems theory to the USM's course redesign story reveals how the three complex adaptive systems leadership capacities combined to change behavior patterns and create a culture of academic innovation toward emergent transformative change. There is evidence to support the unifying, generative, and convergent leadership roles that the System played during the eight-year initiative.

Unifying leadership. Hazy (2012) observed that unifying leadership "promotes shared identities and a common ethic to synchronise choices and behaviours across the system" (p. 238). When contextual circumstances change, unifying leadership adapts the system's prevailing identity and ethical posture accordingly—providing system agents with transparency and consistency of purpose as well as predictable rules of interaction. This, then, becomes the attractor or "new normal" for system interactions (see also Hazy, 2008).

Prior to the launch of the E&E initiative in 2003, the USM had already developed a strong sense of identity as an emerging leader in the delivery of high-quality, affordable public higher education. In an August 2002 press release announcing Brit Kirwan's arrival, the new chancellor claimed that USM institutions were "delivering on their promise to attain national eminence, and have the momentum to take their rightful place among their peer institutions—the North Carolinas, Wisconsins, Michigans, the very best that American public higher education can offer" (USM, 2002).

From the start, the messages coming from the chancellor's office about what the USM's mission would be under Kirwan's leadership were effective, clear, and consistently repeated key phrases intended to inspire action. As the *gatekeepers* of social equity and the nation's economic competitiveness, the System's *moral obligation* and *primary imperative* would be to "build a stronger culture of college completion on our campuses" (Kirwan, 2013). Kirwan regularly characterized the USM's mission as *urgent* and our *awesome responsibility* to the nation. To achieve its mission, the "new normal" for USM institutions beginning in 2003 was to become both more *effective* and *efficient*, offering high-quality degree programs at a lower cost.

Boal and Schultz (2007) have argued that, through consistent messaging, unifying leadership plays a crucial role in shaping "the shared meanings that provide the rationale by which the past, present, and the future of the organization coalesce" (p. 411). These kinds of personalized appeals establish purpose through symbolic key words or "tags" within messages that rally members and mobilize them for unified action—ultimately influencing agent interactions and aligning activity toward convergence around the achievement of system goals (see also Holland, 1995; Surie & Hazy, 2006).

Convergent leadership. Within complex adaptive systems theory, the activities, objectives, and rewards that are chosen to achieve the purpose toward which the system is converging comprise convergent leadership (Goldstein & Hazy, 2006). According to Hazy (2006), convergent leadership enables a complex adaptive system to approach a "dynamical system attractor" and come closer to a state of relative stability.

In this way, the USM's 2003 E&E initiative began largely as a convergent activity, aimed at making incremental improvements in existing structures to improve effectiveness and efficiency—the System's new "structural attractor." In addition to the E&E strategies aimed at garnering more competitive procurement contracting and decreasing energy costs, academic E&E initiatives included increasing faculty workload (measured in terms of courses), decreasing students' time to degree, and growing enrollments. Work on the E&E projects progressed largely through existing structures and procedures. By the end of its first year in 2004, the E&E initiative reported a total of $65.5 million in cost savings or avoidance, reallocation of funds, and entrepreneurial revenue. Consequently, the System had the resources available to invest $500,000 in support of the initial course redesign work.

Perhaps even more important, however, was the role that convergent leadership of the System office played in garnering the support of the USM's existing "market" for resources, the state government. While Maryland's Republican governor Robert Ehrlich and its majority Democrat General Assembly agreed over very little during Ehrlich's tenure (2003–2007), higher education remained one of the "Five Pillars" of the state's economic development plans, largely due to the System's concerted efforts and documented successes in being good stewards of taxpayer money. By 2006, the state had demonstrated its support of the USM's college completion mission by—among other things—doubling need-based financial aid and steadily increasing the USM's budget to account for enrollment growth and providing resources to the System's historically Black campuses (Mills, 2006). Savings from E&E and the good will generated between the USM and the state's government continues to this day.

Thus, convergent leadership in the USM involved more than simply managing or administering the System in its current state. Rather, it comprised "direction and change over time toward some purpose" and "catalytic action" aimed at providing system agents with the guidance they needed to take action, make decisions, and exploit existing resources (Hazy, 2008, p. 364). But, as Uhl-Bien and colleagues (2007) cautioned, convergent leadership must always be exercised in consideration of the impact that too much efficiency can have on a system's flexibility to find ways to adapt to a changing environment.

Generative leadership. As discussed earlier, generative problem-solving in complex adaptive systems is achieved through social networks rather than by groups coordinated by centralized authorities. Complex adaptive systems require new and different types of leadership using indirect mechanisms that increase information flow and interaction rates (Mumford & Licuanan, 2004; Uhl-Bien et al., 2007). According to Hazy (2011), "this catalyzing of cross-functional communication, learning, and exploration of the environment in turn generates new ideas and possibilities for the overall system" (p. 173).

The launch of the USM's course redesign initiative in 2006 marked a shift to a more generative role for the System. For the first time, the Board of Regents and the USM office became directly involved in promoting the systemwide development and testing of a teaching and learning innovation aimed at collecting actionable knowledge about how to address high DFW rates in "gateway" courses. To respond to changes in the environment and achieve "creative problem-solving," the System used existing structured social networks and consistent and constant communication to increase dialogue and collaboration, which generated new ideas and possibilities. Regular conversations at the standing meetings of the presidents, provosts, chief information officers, and other key leadership positions kept the academic innovation topic on the agenda. System staff also generated new networks such as the faculty fellows as well as virtual networks of instructional technology support staff, directors of the teaching and learning centers, and others interested generally in academic change. The networks generated through the project gradually created trusted channels for development of common terminology, quicker sharing of proven practices, new collaborative projects, and other forms of mutual support. Over time, these discussions helped to change the conversation from being just about course redesign to becoming more about academic innovation broadly. We found, as Boal and Schultz (2007) observed, that dialogue helped to build shared meanings and collective pools of knowledge that promoted "perspective making, taking, and shaping" (p. 417).

At the same time, System office officials were careful to manage the generative work that was occurring in order to focus and direct attention. Rather than to mandate systemwide change, for example, the course redesign project was deliberately designed to reduce complexity and garner buy-in from key stakeholders by engaging in only a small set of redesigns that were structured first as pilots, then as full implementations. As a result, the USM was in a much better position to determine the real value of the academic innovations and recommend models to our faculty that were proven to effect truly meaningful change for our students. As Surie and Hazy (2006) cautioned, it is important to "limit the impact of interactions to a subset of the system when conducting experiments, and thus limit the consequences of mistakes or underdeveloped ideas that may result in complexity catastrophes" (p. 18).

Thus, generative leadership during the course redesign project catalyzed interactions that identified new directions and explored new resources for the System as well. So, rather than to be just about leading "innovation," generative activities also included evaluation, selection, and partitioning to reduce the negative consequences of failed experiments. Surie and Hazy (2006) argued that, in this way, generative leadership in a complex adaptive system involves creating the rich, interactive context necessary for innovation to occur while reducing or absorbing the complexity that might otherwise overwhelm the system and its agents.

LESSONS LEARNED

According to Eoyang and Olson (2001), there are three ways in which a system can change from an existing attractor to another. The first is disruption, which forces system agents out of their traditional ways of doing things and requires them to innovate. This disruptive approach often leads to resistance, however, as agents in the system feel increasingly threatened or insecure and become even more attached to old behavior patterns. The second approach identifies the need, defines the desired performance, and develops plans to bridge the gap between the current state and envisioned future.

While this visionary approach is hopeful, planful, and intentional, the gaps identified are frequently based on current patterns "so, without intending to, they reinforce the behaviors of the past rather than those of the preferred future" (Eoyang & Olson, 2001, p. 3). The third approach to shifting system attractors is to intentionally build bridges between the existing and new attractors by identifying old behaviors to be carried over into the new patterns. While this tack requires more effort and clear communication of expectations to avoid confusion, the security provided by the continuity builds agents' confidence at the same time that stepwise and systematic inquiry clarifies which behaviors need to be kept and which need to be eliminated. While the USM's shift to a culture of academic innovation was achieved largely through this third approach, the process was not without its flaws.

First, the USM's course redesign initiative was, by itself, largely a generative activity, which may help to explain why institutionalization of course redesign across the System institutions has not been particularly transformative in and of itself. After the initial "call to action" from the chancellor, for example, more unifying leadership would have helped to clarify outcomes from the project and create unified metrics for assessment. Similarly, stronger unifying leadership might have strengthened ties between the generative course redesign activities and convergent activities aimed at increasing efficiencies. Data on the cost savings from course redesign were only occasionally collected, and there was little discussion of and how that return on the System's investment might be exploited to sustain the redesigned courses or fund more academic innovation activities. Likewise, academic "managers" such as program coordinators and department chairs were largely left out of the discussions. As a result, when the initiative ended, there was very little department chair support or understanding, and the conditions were not in place to allow the changes to be sustained.

Second, as a generative activity, the USM did little to curate and disseminate the insights from the course redesign initiative. Unfortunately, the project did not enforce a very systematic evaluation in order to make comparisons and draw valid conclusions from them. While we finally did so retrospectively, the data from these experiments should have been synthesized and leveraged throughout the project to help generate new ideas and tap into new resources for additional innovation activity. According to Surie and Hazy (2006), it is important that generative leaders "ensure that this resource is leveraged effectively by retaining and reusing knowledge or ideas generated through such interactions in other interactions in a wide variety of contexts" (p. 18). In the future, it will be important that System-led generative activities help institutions to collect data in a format that makes it easier to compare experiences and set priorities within and across institutions.

Surie and Hazy (2006) suggested the creation of "centers of excellence" as a way to (a) leverage insights generated from innovation by diffusing and reusing them in as many new projects as possible and (b) absorb complexity by codifying and replicating knowledge. This is, in fact, the role that the Kirwan Center has evolved into since its creation in 2013. Additionally, the center is increasingly playing a unifying leadership role, working in support of the generative leadership on the campuses coming out of the ATAC and CPFD groups by removing barriers (policies, procedures, facilities) and creating opportunities (collaborations, funded projects, and the like).

CONCLUSION

While we have generated a great deal of momentum around academic innovation within the USM, the path has been neither quick nor easy—there is still much left to do. We have learned that change takes time and is often contingent on garnering additional and sustained support, which state higher education systems are often in a unique position to request from the state or other potential funders. But the USM has also discovered that the system office can play a key role in facilitating lasting and meaningful change through active leadership, initiatives, and strategies that enable a culture of academic innovation across its constituent institutions.

In an increasingly difficult climate for higher education, complex adaptive systems theory appears to hold promise for explaining this culture-changing leadership role that state systems can play. Reframing within a complex adaptive systems paradigm will require, however, that state systems move beyond simply articulating a vision, strategy, and objectives to "mobilize the troops." Transformative change requires the creation of the structure and context for system members to provide diverse perspectives and focus attention on multiple dimensions of the problem. The state system can no longer merely be the gatherer, interpreter, and synthesizer of feedback that then heroically converts the information into a strategy or vision. Instead, feedback needs to be channeled back through the organization's members who are in the best position to interpret and synthesize the new information into ever more usable models of the environment. And, finally, state systems can no longer evaluate progress of an innovation on its perceived contribution to a predetermined strategy. The progress of new innovations must be evaluated on their own terms through evolutionary selection—the ability to learn continuously and implement learning in action as the project proceeds.

Cilliers (1998) suggested that there is a difference between a system that is *complex* as compared to one that is merely *complicated*. If a system can be described in terms of its individual parts, then it is just complicated. A complex system, by contrast, cannot be fully understood simply by analyzing its components. In other words, the whole of the system is greater than the sum of its parts. Perhaps through a better understanding of these complex dynamics and the role of the state system's potential leadership capacities within that context, we can enable stronger innovation cultures on our campuses that will lead to truly transformative change in higher education.

CHAPTER 7 TAKEAWAYS

- Course redesign can be an important tool for improving the learning experiences of students.

- Create mechanisms to collect and utilize data throughout the innovation effort.

- Lack of a sustained leadership and continuous communication can create barriers to fostering buy-in and sustainability.

- Developing backbone mechanisms can be critical for collecting and distributing insights from the innovation effort as well as serve as crucial support for maintaining momentum around the innovation.

NOTES

1. The USM does not include the 16 community colleges in Maryland, although the Maryland community colleges' appropriations are based on a percentage of the USM budget, creating an important and durable link. The leadership of the USM and the Maryland Association of Community Colleges (MACC) meet on a regular basis and work cooperatively for state support of higher education with regard to policy, regulation, and state resources. Additionally, given that nearly one-third of the students entering USM institutions are Maryland community college transfers, these two higher education sectors work closely on transfer policies and practices.
2. We will continue to use the upper-case "System" to refer to the USM and the lower-case "system" when referring to this broader definition of a system, particularly the broader population of higher education systems comprised of multiple campuses under a single governing board.
3. Some authors, including Eoyang and Holladay (2013), prefer the term *container* to describe these boundaries on system action.
4. Uhl-Bien and associates (2007) also identified three similar types of leadership capacities within complex adaptive systems, which they called "adaptive," "enabling," and "administrative."

REFERENCES

Ashby, W. R. (1962). Principles of the self-organizing system. In H. von Foerster & G. W. Zoph (Eds.), *Principles of self-organization: Transactions of the University of Illinois symposium on self-organization* (pp. 255–278). Pergamon Press.

Banathy, B. H. (1991). *Systems design of education: A journey to create the future*. Englewood Educational Technology.

Boal, K. B., & Schultz, P. L. (2007). Storytelling, time, and evolution: The role of strategic leadership in complex adaptive systems. *Leadership Quarterly, 18*, 411–428. doi:10.1016/j.leaqua.2007.04.008

Child, J., & McGrath, R. G. (2001). Organizations unfettered: Organizational form in an information-intensive economy. *Academy of Management Journal, 44*, 1135–1149. doi:10.2307/3069393

Cilliers, P. (1998). *Complexity and postmodernism: Understanding complex systems.* Routledge.

Eckel, P. D., Hill, B., & Green, M. (1998). *On change: En route to transformation* (American Council on Education Occasional Paper). http://files.eric.ed.gov/fulltext/ED435293.pdf

Ehrmann, S. C., & Bishop, M. J. (2015). *Pushing the barriers to teaching improvement: A state system's experience with faculty-led, technology-supported course redesign.* William E. Kirwan Center for Academic Innovation, University System of Maryland. http://www.usmd.edu/cai/sites/default/files/USMCourseRedesign-Report-Sept2015.pdf

Eoyang, G. H., & Holladay, R. J. (2013). *Adaptive action: Leveraging uncertainty in your organization.* Stanford Business Books.

Eoyang, G. H., & Olson, E. (2001). *AI: Path to a new attractor.* Appreciative Inquiry Commons. https://appreciativeinquiry.case.edu/research/bibPapersDetail.cfm?coid=760

Geiger, R. L. (2010). Impact of the financial crisis on higher education in the United States. *International Higher Education, 59,* 9–11. http://ejournals.bc.edu/ojs/index.php/ihe/issue/view/835

Goldstein, J., & Hazy, J. K. (2006). Editorial introduction to the special issue: From complexity to leadership and back to complexity. *Emergence: Complexity and Organization, 8*(4), v–vii. http://emergentpublications.com/ECO/ECO_other/Issue_8_4_1_ED.pdf

Hall, A. D., & Fagen, R. E. (1956). Definition of system. *General Systems, 1,* 81–92.

Hazy, J. K. (2008). Patterns of leadership: A case study of influence signaling in an entrepreneurial firm. In M. Uhl-Bien & R. Marion (Eds.), *Complexity leadership: Part I, conceptual foundations* (pp. 379–417). Information Age.

Hazy, J. K. (2011). Parsing the "influential increment" in the language of complexity: Uncovering systemic mechanisms of leadership influence. *Journal of Complexity in Leadership and Management, 1,* 116–132. doi:10.1504/ijclm.2011.040735

Hazy, J. K. (2012). The unifying function of leadership: Shaping identity, ethics and the local rules of interaction. *International Journal of Society Systems Science, 4,* 222–241. doi:10.1504/IJSSS.2012.047990

Hazy, J. K., Ashley, A. S., Moskalev, S. A., & Torras, M. (2011). Technology leverage and sustainable society systems: A call for technology forecasting that anticipates innovation. *International Journal of Society Systems Science, 3*, 5–20. doi:10.1504/IJSSS.2011.038930

Hazy, J. K., Moskalev, S. A., & Torras, M. (2010). Mechanisms of social value creation: Extending financial modeling to social entrepreneurship and social innovation. *International Journal of Society Systems Science, 2*, 134–157. doi:10.1504/IJSSS.2010.032572

Hazy, J. K., & Uhl-Bien, M. (2014). Changing the rules: The implications of complexity science for leadership research and practice. In D. V. Day (Ed.), *The Oxford Handbook of Leadership and Organizations* (pp. 709–732). Oxford University Press.

Hirsch, M. W., Smale, S., & Devaney, R. L. (2004). *Differential equations, dynamical systems, and an introduction to chaos* (2nd ed.). Elsevier.

Holland, J. H. (1995). *Hidden order: How adaptation builds complexity*. Addison-Wesley.

Ilinitch, A. Y., D'Aveni, R. A., & Lewin, A. Y. (1996). New organizational forms and strategies for managing in hypercompetitive environments. *Organization Science, 7*, 211–220. doi:10.1287/orsc.7.3.211

Keshavarz, N., Nutbeam, D., Rowling, L., & Khavarpour, F. (2010). Schools as social complex adaptive systems: A new way to understand the challenges of introducing the health promoting schools concept. *Social Science & Medicine, 70*, 1467–1474. doi:10.1016/j.socscimed.2010.01.034

Kezar, A., & Eckel, P. D. (2002a). The effect of institutional culture on change strategies in higher education: Universal principles or culturally responsive concepts? *Journal of Higher Education, 73*, 435–460. doi:10.1353/jhe.2002.0038

Kezar, A., & Eckel, P. D. (2002b). Examining the institutional transformation process: The importance of sensemaking and inter-related strategies. *Research in Higher Education, 43*, 295–328. doi:10.1023/A:1014889001242

Kirwan, W. E. (2013, April 15). How we can be better stewards of the American dream. *Chronicle of Higher Education*. http://chronicle.com/article/How-We-Can-Be-Better-Stewards/138503/

Lane, J. E. (2013). Higher education systems 3.0: Adding value to states and institutions. In J. E. Lane & D. B. Johnstone (Eds.),

Higher education systems 3.0: Harnessing systemness, delivering performance (pp. 3–26). State University of New York Press.

Levin, B., & Fullan, M. (2008). Learning about system renewal. *Educational Management and Leadership, 36,* 289–304. doi:10.1177/1741143207087778

Mills, K. (2006). "Effectiveness and efficiency": The University System of Maryland's campaign to control costs and increase student aid. *National CrossTalk, 14*(2). National Center for Public Policy and Higher Education. http://www.highereducation.org/crosstalk/ctbook/pdfbook/MarylandEffectivenessBookLayout.pdf

Mumford, M. D., & Licuanan, B. (2004). Leading for innovation: Conclusions, issues, and directions. *Leadership Quarterly, 15,* 163–171. doi:10.1016/j.leaqua.2003.12.010

Reschke, C. H., Bogenhold, D., & Kraus, S. (2010). How innovation and entrepreneurship can conquer uncertainty and complexity: Learning about the unexpected. *International Journal of Complexity in Leadership and Management, 1,* 55–71. doi:10.1504/IJCLM.2010.035789

Surie, G., & Hazy, J. K. (2006). Generative leadership: Nurturing innovation in complex systems. *Emergence: Complexity and Organization, 8*(4), 13–26.

Uhl-Bien, M., Marion, R., & McKelvey, B. (2007). Complexity leadership theory: Shifting leadership from the industrial age to the knowledge era. *Leadership Quarterly, 18,* 298–318. doi:10.1016/j.leaqua.2007.04.002

University System of Maryland (USM). (2002). USM Chancellor "Brit" Kirwan to begin August 1 [Press release]. http://www.usmd.edu/newsroom/2002Releases/kirwan.html

University System of Maryland Board of Regents. (2010). *Powering Maryland forward: USM's 2020 plan for more degrees, a stronger innovation economy, a higher quality of life.* http://www.usmd.edu/10yrplan/USM2020.pdf

Zimpher, N. L. (2013). Systemness: Unpacking the value of higher education systems. In J. E. Lane & D. B. Johnstone (Eds.), *Higher education systems 3.0: Harnessing systemness, delivering performance* (pp. 27–44). State University of New York Press.

Part IV

FRAMEWORKS FOR LARGE-SCALE CHANGE

8

DRIVING STUDENT SUCCESS COLLECTIVELY

Lessons Scaling from Campuses to Systems to a Network of Systems

REBECCA R. MARTIN AND JASON E. LANE

ABSTRACT

Increasing college attainment and closing equity gaps are nationwide priorities, with widely recognized benefits for individuals, the economy, and civil society. Exemplars of student success have emerged across higher education institutions, systems, and states; but national completion rates continue to rise only slightly, and equity gaps continue to widen. A contributing factor is that higher education too often focuses on isolated impacts, seeking to create new interventions rather than scaling what works across the campus, across multiple campuses, or across multiple networks of campuses. This chapter examines the efforts of the National Association of System Heads (NASH) to work across multiple higher education systems in order to create a focused and scaled effort to improve student success and increase completion rates across the United States. Lessons for collaboration are extrapolated and shared.

A cross the United States, increasing college completion and closing equity gaps have emerged as a top priority for higher education institutions and higher education systems. Despite headlines that question the value of college degrees, evidence shows that such credentials yield vast benefits, including healthier, wealthier, more socially mobile students; reduced costs to institutions; and economic gains to states and communities. Under the Obama administration, increasing college completion and increasing success among historically under-represented populations became a national imperative, with major foundations and associations shifting their focus to attempt to address this issue. Yet the national completion rate barely moved.

Of course, funders and associations do not graduate students. Colleges and universities do. Some institutions were incredibly effective in advancing new strategies for increasing completion rates, often working with external funders. Yet, these efforts too often remained isolated, affecting too few students to have an impact on the national numbers. There are hundreds of examples of programs across the United States that have had isolated impacts on improving student persistence, but these victories have yet to materially impact national completion rates. Best practices and lessons learned have, for the most part, remained with individual institutions. As a result, this institutional-based focus has led to limited codification of cost data, analysis impact, and sharing of key successes (Lane, 2018).

There need to be ways to harness the aggregate resources of the sector to create change and build a model of higher education that can better respond to the needs of today's students. To affect substantive change, higher education needs to take more of a collective impact approach. That is, campuses need to find ways to collaborate with each other to share best practices, better leverage resources, and develop structures that support students as they progress toward a high-quality credential. The argument of this volume is that multicampus higher education systems are a natural mechanism for facilitating such collective work.

The efforts described in the previous chapters focus on how individual systems have worked to scale interventions across campus and create communities of practice to share knowledge among multiple institutions. But what if we scaled these efforts to create a system of systems working together?

THE SYSTEM'S ROLE IN STUDENT SUCCESS

While the national agenda for college completion is gaining momentum, it is clear that most of the levers for driving the necessary changes rest with the states (Kelly & Schneider, 2012; Perna & Finney, 2014). Legally and practically, state governments retain primary authority over higher education in the United States. This is particularly relevant for the public sector. Governance mechanisms are created by the states. Funding, at least partially, is provided by states. Rules and regulations about academic programs and credit mobility are created and enforced by states. Incentives (and disincentives) for change can be advanced by states. And elected officials can set priorities for the public tertiary sector.

At the same time, policymakers and institutional leaders are looking for a playbook of proven strategies that can promote student success and institutional performance, as well as approaches for scaling up successful reform efforts (Kelly & Schneider, 2012). For example, enhanced student pathways that support student transfer, outcome-based funding that incentivizes institutional action, and state policy leadership that sets a bold vision for change all hold promise in this regard.

One lever that has been underutilized by states is multicampus governance models, often referred to as state systems of higher education. This type of governance was created as a means to improve coordination and regulation of public higher education in the state (see chapter 1). However, these systems have only recently begun to play a leadership role in advancing student success across their campuses. The other chapters in this volume detail some of these efforts.

Indeed, public university systems are uniquely positioned to harness the collective efforts of their institutions. With direct influence over campus leadership and resource allocations, as well as responsibility for academic programs and policy development, system governing boards and administrations have the capacity to set a strategic agenda for their constituent institutions. This work involves translating state-level vision into campus-level action using approaches such as goal setting, action plans, accountability measures, and governing board support (Bensimon et al., 2012). Equally important is the potential to build consensus across campuses to bring about transformational change in the ways in which instruction is designed and delivered.

As discussed in the other chapters, system-led student success initiatives do present challenges for their leaders. Some campuses will not want to fully participate, with priorities such as graduate education and institutional specialization competing for resources. Others may chafe at the system role in what they see as the campus prerogative. A key component of system work in this area is to facilitate collaboration, while also respecting and honoring diversification.

With increasing competition among institutions, systems have the capacity to act in the best interests of their students, setting aside individual campuses' interests and turf battles. As detailed in the chapters in this volume, some systems have incentivized processes for innovation and reform, with campus-based initiatives driven through system leadership. By creating space for innovation and reform through structures and policies, they create a safe space for the inevitable failure that is necessary to develop viable models for multiple campuses and bring about real change (Crandall & Soares, 2015). In short, systems have the ability to "behave in a way that is more powerful and impactful than what can be achieved by individual campuses acting alone" (Zimpher, 2013, p. 27).

MOVING TO A NETWORK OF SYSTEMS

While systems have the ability to coordinate among multiple campuses, these efforts remain largely constrained by state borders. To scale efforts toward a national movement, there need to be ways to coordinate among multiple systems. Much like campuses can benefit by working with each other, systems can also benefit from working with one another. As such the benefits of collective action to improve completion rates and close equity gaps can be increased exponentially across the country.

Unlike systems that have a legal governing entity to oversee the coordination of their campuses, there is no such governance entity for multiple systems. However, in 1979, leaders of several such systems created the National Association of System Heads (NASH), a professional organization that serves as a convener of system leaders and an organizer of multisystem initiatives. As such, NASH has emerged as a natural entity for facilitating work across many systems.

While there have been some collective efforts to increase completion rates across systems, nothing has been attempted at the scale that a collective of public university systems could achieve. NASH member institutions, which enroll more than 5.6 million students and serve approximately 75 percent of the US undergraduate student body in public four-year institutions, have the scale and influence to have an unprecedented positive effect on college completion. A firm commitment to identifying and implementing successful completion initiatives across multicampus systems could affect millions of students across 44 systems in 35 states. If completion rates increase by only 5 percent across NASH systems, 50,000 more students would attain degrees each year, leading to over $50 billion in additional income from just one cohort of students over the course of their lifetimes, not to mention indirect benefits associated with improved health, lower crime rates, and overall better quality of life (Julian, 2012).

This chapter focuses on lessons derived from efforts to take this collaboration up to the next level—working across multiple higher education systems to scale best practices across the nation. It examines three efforts advanced by the National Association of System Heads that focus on system-level efforts to advance student success and extrapolate lessons for multicampus and multisystem collaborations. The first effort focused on advancing a particular goal, closing equity gaps, but allowed systems to work in isolation from each other. The second effort advanced one particular intervention, the high-impact practice of undergraduate research, across campuses in six systems and consortia. The third effort took a collective impact approach, targeting evidence-based practices proven to increase completion rates and then creating a network of systems to collectively work together to implement those approaches and share with each other what was learned from their various efforts. Each of these efforts has had varying degrees of success and yielded important clues as to how systems and networks of systems can collaborate to create meaningful change that can positively impact student success.

INITIATIVE 1: ACCESS TO SUCCESS

In 2007, 22 public university systems joined in a concerted effort to boost both the enrollment and the success of low-income students and underrepresented minority students. In the vanguard of the college attainment movement, system heads in this initiative, dubbed *A2S* (Access to Success), agreed to pursue two common goals:

- To increase the number of college graduates in their states

- To ensure that those graduates more broadly represented their state's high school graduates

Specifically, these leaders publicly pledged that by the year 2015 their systems would halve the gaps in college attendance and completion that separate African American, Latino, and American Indian students from White and Asian American students, as well as those between low-income students and more affluent students (Engle et al., 2012).

More than simply committing to a goal, those involved in the A2S network agreed to track their progress along several predetermined metrics. Each year, the systems would report their progress to a central backbone that tracked progress and held the participating systems accountable for reporting their data and making improvements in line with the two overarching goals. These data, however, focused on the specific elements of the A2S goals and were not the same data being tracked by the National Center for Education Statistics' (NCES) Integrated Postsecondary Education Data System (IPEDS). That is, IPEDS reports graduation rates based on first-time, full-time students, which covered only about 58 percent of students when A2S kicked off (Engle & Lynch, 2009). Instead, systems in A2S reported on graduation rates of *all* students regardless of status. Second, IPEDS disaggregates graduation rates based on race, but not based on social-economic factors. The A2S systems committed to both.

In this effort, the Education Trust and the National Association of System Heads (NASH) served as the organizational backbone for the effort. A2S represented the potential to scale impact across the nation. The 22 systems[1] that participated in the effort represented 312 two-year and four-year campuses. These campuses served approximately 3.5 million students annually, including nearly two out of five students of color and low-income students enrolled in public four-year institutions in the United States.

The leaders of this effort carefully monitored and tracked the performance of each system, including analyzing data, interviewing system and campus leaders, and working directly with implementation teams within the system. Important factors in more successful systems include long-term visible leadership, clearly articulated goals at the system and campus levels, and intentional data tracking. Useful tools, such as the use of leading indicators and more strategically using data analysis to drive decision-making, emerged from high-performing institutions (Yeado et al., 2014). A subset of these systems engaged in a network that focused on turning strategic plans into implementation plans and developing foundational strategy at the system level to ensure the continuity of attainment and gap-closing goals during leadership and governance changes (Engle et al., 2012).

Access goals in many of the partnering systems were achieved, particularly for low-income students, though progress toward attainment goals has been slower. By 2014, specific findings across the network included:

Access

- Enrollment for Pell and underrepresented minority students increased in both two- and four-year institutions; the share these students represented in each student body also increased.

- Increases in Pell enrollments at four-year institutions outpaced increases in low-income high school graduates, so access goals were met.

- Increases in underrepresented minority students at four-year institutions did not significantly outpace these increases in high school graduates, so gap goals were not met.

- At two-year institutions, access goals were met for Pell and underrepresented minority students.

Success

- In four-year institutions, success rates for Pell and underrepresented minority students increased.

- Gains were bigger for non-Pell and nonminority students, so gaps generally widened at four-year institutions.

- At two-year institutions, success rates for Pell and under-represented students decreased slightly.

- No progress was made in gap-closing at two-year institutions.

The bottom line was that more Pell and underrepresented minority students entered institutions in the A2S network and made it through with degrees. But the transformation results were not at the level that would have been realized with gap closing on the success front (Education Trust, 2014).

INITIATIVE 2: A SYSTEMS APPROACH TO ENHANCING AND EXPANDING UNDERGRADUATE RESEARCH

The Council on Undergraduate Research (CUR) has a longstanding workshop program to help campus leaders institutionalize undergraduate research initiatives. This practice of undergraduate research is considered a high-impact practice and can be directly linked to improved retention and graduation rates, particularly for students from underrepresented backgrounds and those with low GPAs (Gregerman et al., 1998; Hu et al., 2008). This effort was originally designed as a means for assisting individual campuses. However, in order to expand the potential benefits at a faster rate, CUR expanded their workshops to include representatives from multicampus networks, including public systems of higher education as well as consortia of public and private institutions.

This initiative, unlike A2S, focused on utilizing multicampus collaborations to scale an evidence-based practice for improving undergraduate student success. With financial support from the National Science Foundation and engagement from NASH and the Wabash College Center for Inquiry, CUR designed a new program to improve the quality of undergraduate education at each of the constituent campuses within the six participating systems and consortia.

This workshop program was fundamentally designed to improve the quality of undergraduate education at each of the constituent campuses by leveraging the synergy, influence, and power of the systems and consortia. Curricula were tailored to meet the needs of each system/consortium with such topics as understanding and changing institutional culture, faculty hiring, tenure/promotion and workload issues, curriculum case studies, assessment, funding, supporting nontraditional students, connecting undergraduate research to service learning, community-based learning and international education, and promoting it in all disciplines. Campus and system participants met twice over the course of a year to strengthen implementation and assess progress (Malachowski et al., 2015).

Although their approaches varied, several systems emerged from this project with promising models. The Pennsylvania State System of Higher Education, for example, linked undergraduate research directly to their priorities for improving student success and reducing achievement gaps, providing consistent senior leadership at the system and board levels. The University of Wisconsin System used a distributed leadership model, with system and campus leaders collaborating on a systemwide effort. The California State University System employed a systemic model for implementing high-impact practices on campuses by creating a system-level office and support staff that funds and coordinates dedicated positions on each campus (Gagliardi et al., 2015; California State University, Office of the Chancellor, 2014)).

As part of this project, an analysis of the six participating systems and consortia was conducted to explore the impact of system-based approaches on the implementation and scaling of undergraduate research at the campus level (Malachowski et al., 2015). This analysis included a review of the factors that influence the capacity of systems and consortia to develop and extend these programs, in an effort to inform future system efforts at scaling such reforms. Interviews with key leaders at both the systems/consortia and their campuses, as well as content analysis of the proposals and reports contributed to this review.

The following cross-cutting themes were identified:

- Because of the existence of a centralized administrative backbone, systems and consortia were well positioned to initiate and coordinate multicampus projects.

- Due to their centralized position, systems and consortia are adept at communicating the benefits of collective impact to stakeholders, particularly those in the external environment.

- Implementation necessitated campus leadership buy-in and commitment to fully engaging in activities that both support campus work and support the larger collaborative network.

- Trying to engage campuses that were not fully committed to the work proved to be a distraction and, in some cases, a deterrent to the work. Preference was found for working with a "coalition of the willing."

- Communication is a two-way street. System and consortium offices have limited knowledge of what is happening on constituent campuses. Campuses do not easily understand the larger vision of the collaboration. It takes focused and continual communication from all actors to support a dynamic and sustainable network.

- Building of a collaborative, multicampus team proved to help mitigate the risk of declining resource and changes in senior leadership by creating a peer-support structure, leveraging economies of scale to reduce costs, and creating a framework to introduce network priorities to new senior leaders.

The lessons from this initiative would prove insightful for building a future network of systems to advance student completion.

INITIATIVE 3: TAKING STUDENT SUCCESS TO SCALE (TS3)

To make real improvement in completion levels, NASH leaders recognized the need to act as a collective of collectives—essentially creating a network improvement community among higher education systems. The idea was to take a collective impact approach to create a network of systems committed to implementing evidence-based practices across multiple campuses with the goal of significantly increasing the number of students earning quality educational credentials, particularly students from at-risk backgrounds. The NASH Board invited system leaders to propose evidence-based practices that could be scaled and three were selected to be at the heart of the new network: predictive analytics, high-impact practices, and redesigned math pathways.[2] These three interventions were being scaled up in at least one NASH system with solid evidence of impact on retention, persistence, and completion, while closing equity gaps. The new network became known as Taking Student Success to Scale (TS3) and had 23 member systems as of the end of 2017.

While both previously described initiatives (i.e., A2S and the CUR project) showed promise, they were not without challenges. Systems in the A2S initiative chose divergent strategies to address the commonly identified goals, diluting their potential impact on outcomes. While early commitment from system leaders was clear, campuses were slower to get on board. Individual campuses were more actively engaged in CUR's undergraduate research project, but limitations in system-level knowledge of actual campus circumstances and activities impeded progress. Building on lessons from the A2S and scaling undergraduate research initiatives, the decision was made to promote completion with a holistic and integrated strategy that includes insight and data on what is working best for which students (and at what cost); a playbook of high-quality, proven interventions that can be mapped to specific student needs and institutional capabilities; and effective implementation of best practices. However, unlike the other initiatives, the emerging network focused on scaling practices also had difficulty attracting support from funders and other organizations.

What was also different about the TS3 network is that it emerged out of a sense of urgency to transform how, as a nation, we approach the issue of completion. Funders, states, and systems had often taken an isolated impact approach—investing in and supporting new initiatives at campus level with limited engagement in scaling evidence-based practices across campuses. Rather than seeking to create a "new" intervention, the focus of the network was on utilizing the legal authority of systems to convene and incentivize the work of campuses to implement these proven practices with the goal of significantly moving the national dial on completion.

The network started with the leadership of three systems, California State University System, Tennessee Board of Regents, and the State University of New York. Each of the three lead systems had served as a laboratory for innovation, a hub for analysis, and a gatherer of organizational and environmental intelligence (Gagliardi, 2015). Limited funding from Lumina Foundation was made available to support an initial convening of the network. That first convening attracted more than 150 participants from 20 systems for a two-day summit. The feedback from both system and campus leaders was that they valued the opportunity to learn from each other and create a support network of like-minded colleagues interested in increasing student completion rates. The problem was that the network did not have the funding to sustain itself.

Funders proved to be skeptical of the value of such a network of a system of systems. However, system leaders remained deeply committed to the work and believed there was great value in such a system. So a call went out for interested systems to make a one-time financial commitment to support the early development of the network. Fifteen systems initially stepped forward to provide the financial backing. A steering committee of system and campus leaders was created to guide the network.

The network would eventually evolve to become a community of practice of committed system and campus leaders with a shared vision and mission of implementing these interventions toward a goal of increasing student completion rates. While the work happened on campuses, the network provided a connection and created an environment where those involved were also focused on the overall success of those in the network. The network members voluntarily hosted webinars, shared resources, and even formed peer evaluation teams to provide on-the-ground support to systems in need.[3] The limited resource made available by the partners, which by the end of 2017 had grown to 23 systems, was reserved to hire outside expertise for assistance with data collection and analysis and offsetting the cost of the annual convenings, which continued to attract large groups of participants.

One of the foundational commitments of the network was to work within existing interventions and practices. This included the collection of data. Rather than creating a new reporting scheme, the network committed to use existing data to track success. Since the goal of the effort was to increase completion, it was decided that this would be the overall measure of success. Even though it would not be possible to attribute causality in changes in completion numbers without more detailed data, watching the overall trend would indicate whether systems were moving in the right direction. And since the interventions have already been proven to positively impact completion, it could be inferred that changes in completion would, at least partially, contribute to increases in completions. Again, the intent was to keep the focus on the work and the overall goal, while not drawing institutional resources away for more detailed data reporting.

One of the most innovative aspects of this network was that it sought to tackle a messy and complex goal of increasing completion. Discussions were designed to be informed by data with a focus on sharing best practices and collectively identifying and overcoming barriers. While agreeing on three interventions that were proven to affect completion rates in a positive direction, systems and campuses were left to implement the interventions in a way that best addressed the diversity of campuses and the student population. In fact, the size and scope of the TS3 network allowed campuses to benefit from learning from similar campus types in other systems. Moreover, the networked communities were purposefully comprised of both system and campus representatives; this allowed for knowledge sharing across perspectives and brought greater coherence and greater cooperation between system and campus representatives. The NASH TS3 network provides a common platform to implement tested interventions and measure their impact on student achievement for all types of systems and institutions involved in the initiative. This effort will support the dual promise of access and opportunity for all students who wish to pursue higher learning, especially those from underrepresented minority and low-income backgrounds. By creating a platform for shared implementation experiences, and by using volunteer systems and institutions as test sites for the adoption and analysis of each of the three chosen interventions, the TS3 networked improvement community has been strengthened on behalf of the students and communities served, particularly those who are in greatest need.

As of this writing, the network is only three years in operation. What began as three initial systems has grown to a network of 23 systems with the potential to influence approximately than 2.5 million undergraduate students on more than 300 campuses. Moreover, while funding was difficult to come by in the early days, the network has now received funding from the Lumina Foundation and the Bill & Melinda Gates Foundation to support the high-impact practices and predictive analytics, respectively. While the jury remains out on the impact on long-term completion rates, the network has proven successful in terms of being an unprecedented, national commitment of systems and campuses investing their own resources to collectively work together to improve completion rates.

THE LESSONS FROM THE COLLECTIVE IMPACT OF A NETWORK OF SYSTEMS

The work of the TS3 network closely mirrors the efforts of other large-scale change initiatives that have embraced what Kania and Kramer (2011) have referred to as "collective impact." The primary idea behind collective impact is to bring together a disparate set of actors to focus on creating purposeful change about a complex issue affecting society. This approach has been successfully used by communities across the United States to improve high school graduation rates, address clean drinking water problems, and reduce childhood obesity. Examples of documented success of this approach in the education arena include community-based efforts such as the Strive Partnership in Cincinnati; schools districts in Menomonee Falls, Wisconsin, and Montgomery County, Maryland (Park et al., 2013); and Community College Pathways (Bryk et al., 2015).

By using common definitions of success, sharing learnings, and a common infrastructure, collective impact can be an incredibly powerful tool to drive large-scale change. Like the examples mentioned, the TS3 network possessed no formal authority to advance the work that it championed. Rather it emerged as a national coalition of the willing interested in increasing college completion rates. Moreover, the network was not driven by external funding or a desire to compete for a specific funding opportunity. Instead, the members of the network contributed their own resources to support the work and built momentum toward attracting funding to support the work. What drove the network was the shared commitment toward increasing the number of individuals with a high-quality postsecondary credential and collectively implementing proven practices that would positively affect that goal.

Looking at the TS3 network through the lens of collective impact (Kania & Kramer, 2011) can aid in understanding how the network has sustained itself as well as derive lessons for other collaborative work undertaken by multicampus systems or other shared efforts. Following are the five principals of collective impact applied to the TS3 network:

Common Agenda. The TS3 network created a shared goal of leveraging its scale to implement three evidence-based practices to increase the number of individuals with high-quality postsecondary credentials. This shared goal of contributing to a national priority while utilizing the unique assets of multicampus systems proved to be a unifying vision that has continued to sustain the work of the network. Moreover, the focus on three common evidence-based practices provided a foundation for shared learning and the creation of a community of practice.

Common Progress Measures. The network agreed on one high level of metric, completion, to be the overarching goal and long-term measure of success. Noting that there is a significant lag in terms of the impact of any intervention on completion, the network also focused on the implementation of intervention efforts. This secondary goal assumed that the interventions were already evidenced to have impact and therefore the goal should be to implement what works and not expend additional resources reproving the impact of the interventions.

Mutually Reinforcing Activities. The network focused on a multifaceted approach to engaging network members. This included the development of webinars to keep network members connected as well as using knowledge from more experienced members to develop tools to help more novice campuses through implementation. The network also hosts an annual convening where member systems are invited to send a team of campus and system leaders to a two-day change leadership workshop where the team members work with each other and other teams to learn about best practices in terms of implementing the three interventions. There is also a website that serves as a central repository of resources.

Communications. Communicating among the network has been an important part of sustaining the work and keeping network members engaged. In addition to the regular webinars and the webpage repository, there is a monthly teleconference with system leads to keep them updated on network activities. At each teleconference, a system leader is responsible for leading a conversation of relevance to the work of the network. This creates a community of practice among system leaders and keeps them engaged in the network's work.

Backbone Organization. The TS3 network is embedded within the National Association of System Heads, which serves as the administrative backbone for the network. The staff for NASH provide the necessary support through convening of meetings, tracking network member progress, serving as a spokesperson for the network, and providing administrative support for the work. There is also a network steering committee comprised of campus and system leaders committed to guiding, supporting, and engaging the network membership.

The complex challenge of addressing the nation's completion agenda requires multiple levels of networks that break down the organizational silos that for too long have defined how higher education operates. Faculty and staff need to work together on campuses. Campuses need to share resources and knowledge and hold each other accountable. And systems have the unique asset of scale to be able to ramp up interventions in a way no other higher education entity can. While each system is different, we have learned from the TS3 network that there is much to be gained from a network of systems that can learn from each other. Furthermore, the lessons we have learned thus far from the TS3 network can be applied to other collaborations seeking to address the completion challenge.

CONCLUSION

The struggle to close equity gaps and improve student success across public university systems is continuing, with progress coming in fits and starts. As we take successful pilot projects to scale, political processes and culture change will become even more important than technological solutions and resource investments. Active and committed leadership is essential and needs to come from many places in system administration and board governance, as well as on campuses.

Systems have the capacity to leverage their influence across institutions to raise the bar on student success. They can serve as innovation incubators, assisting campuses in building the strategic enrollment and student lifecycle management needed to support education in the twenty-first century (Mintz, 2014). System leaders can shine a light on disaggregated student outcome data to address the varied needs of diverse students. They can empower and support cohorts of campuses that are ready and willing to be more integrated by offering tools, expertise, and incentives to move the agenda forward (Gagliardi, 2015; Lane & Johnstone, 2013). They put the interests of students above campuses, to smooth pathways across system institutions, promoting student mobility and attainment.

What was found from the three initiatives described earlier is that an effective network needs to be comprised of a coalition of the willing—forced involvement can be a distraction. There needs to be shared sense of vision; the network members need to allow for diversity of institutional type and implementation design while holding each other accountable for advancing a shared agenda. In addition, focusing on scaling best practices rather than seeking additional evidence about the efficacy of a particular intervention allows for energy to be focused on sharing best practices and co-learning with each other. Finally, there needs to be a backbone of support that sustains and compels the network forward.

It is imperative that systems keep student success at the forefront of their goals and priorities, especially in this time of shifting resources and political turmoil. Only through a focus on student success can we continue to make good on promoting social mobility and economic growth.

CHAPTER 8 TAKEAWAYS

- TS3 is a network of systems collectively working to implement evidence-based practices that support student success.

- As much as campuses can learn from each other, so too system leaders can form communities of practice to better understand how systems can support the work of campuses.

- Forcing campuses to be involved when they don't want to can create unneeded distractions; there are advantages to starting with a coalition of the willing.

- Shared vision is important for unifying activities across campuses, fostering ownership of the initiative, and keeping everyone moving in the same direction.

- We need to move away from constantly reinventing the wheel when it comes to designing student supports and look to scale up evidence practices that are proven to work across institutional types and diverse sets of students.

NOTES

1. Twenty-four systems originally committed to the initiative, but two dropped out in the early stages of the work.
2. We do not go into great detail about these practices here. Additional information about each intervention can be found in the following location: Predictive Analytics: Denley, 2014; Lane & Finsel, 2014; chapter 5 of this volume; Redesigning Math Pathway: Rodriguez et al., 2016; Denley, 2016; High-Impact Practices: Kuh (2008); California State University, Office of the Chancellor, 2014; chapter 3 of this volume. Additional resources can also be found at the TS3 website: http://ts3.nashonline. org/.

3. The inviting system covered the cost of travel for the peer evaluation team, but the knowledge and time of those individuals was shared freely.

REFERENCES

Bensimon, E. M., Dowd, A. C., Longanecker, D., & Witham, K. (2012). We have goals. Now what? *Change: The Magazine of Higher Learning, 44*(6), 14–25. doi:10.1080/00091383.2012.7 28948

Bryk, A. S., Gomez, L. Grunow, A., & LeMahieu, P. (2015). *Learning to improve: How America's schools can be the best at getting better.* Harvard University Press.

California State University, Office of the Chancellor. (2014). *Invitation to CSU campuses: Preparing to scale high-impact practices* [Memorandum]. http://www.calstate.edu/engage/documents/Invitation-to-CSU-Campuses-Preparing-to-Scale-HIPs.pdf

Crandall, J. R., & Soares, L. (2015). *The architecture of innovation: System-level course redesign in Tennessee.* American Council on Education. https://www.acenet.edu/news-room/Pages/Lumina-System-Level-Course-Redesign.aspx

Engle, J., & Lynch, M. (2009). *Charting a necessary path: The baseline report of public higher education systems in the access to success initiative.* The Education Trust & NASH (National Association of System Heads).

Engle, J., Yeado, J., Brusi, R., & Cruz, J. L. (2012). *Replenishing opportunity in America: The 2012 midterm report of public higher education systems in the access to success initiative.* Education Trust. https://edtrust.org/resource/replenishing-opportunity-in-america/

Gagliardi, J. S. (2015). From perpetuation to innovation: Removing barriers to change in higher education. In J. E. Lane (Ed.), *Higher education reconsidered: Executing change to drive collective impact* (pp. 61–96). State University of New York Press.

Gagliardi, J. S., Martin, R. R., Wise, K., & Blaich, C. (2015). The system effect: Scaling high-impact practices across campuses. *New Directions for Higher Education,* 15–26. doi:10.1002/he.20 119

Gregerman, S. R., Lerner, J. S., von Hippel, W., Jonides, J., & Nagda, B. A. (1998). Undergraduate student-faculty research partnerships affect student retention. *Review of Higher Education, 22*(1), 55–72.

Hu, S., Scheuch, K., Schwartz, R., Gaston Gayles, J., & Li, S. (2008). Reinventing undergraduate education: Engaging college students in research and creative activities. *ASHE Higher Education Report, 33*(4).

Julian, T. (2012). *Work-life earnings by field of degree and occupation for people with a bachelor's degree: 2011.* U.S. Census Bureau. https://www.census.gov/prod/2012pubs/acsbr11-04.pdf

Kania, J., & Kramer, M. (2011). Collective impact. *Stanford Social Innovation Review.* http://ssir.org/articles/entry/collective_impact

Kelly, A. P., & Schneider, B. (2012). *Getting to graduation: The completion agenda in higher education.* Johns Hopkins University Press.

Kuh, G. D. (2008). *High-impact educational practices: What they are, who has access to them, why they matter.* AAC&U.

Lane, J. E. (2018). Data analytics, systemness and predicting student success in college: Examining how the data revolution matters to higher education policy makers. In J. Gagliardi (Eds.), *The higher education data revolution.* Stylus.

Lane, J. E., & Finsel, B. A. (2014). Fostering smarter colleges and universities: Data, big data, and analytics. In J. E. Lane (Ed.), *Building a smarter university: Data, big data, and analytics* (pp. 3–26). State University of New York Press.

Malachowski, M., Osborne, J. M., Karukstis, K. K., & Ambos, E. L. (2015). Realizing student, faculty, and institutional outcomes at scale: Institutionalizing undergraduate research, scholarship, and creative activity within systems and consortia. *New Directions for Higher Education,* 3–13. doi:10.1002/he.20118

Mintz, S. (2014, March 26). The shifting role of university systems [Web log post]. https://www.insidehighered.com/blogs/higher-ed-beta/shifting-role-university-systems

Park, S., Hironaka, S., Carver, P., & Nordstrum, L. (2013). *Continuous improvement in education.* Carnegie Foundation for the Advancement of Teaching. http://www.carnegiefoundation.org/resources/publications/continuous-improvement-education/

Perna, L. W., & Finney, J. E. (2014). *The attainment agenda: State policy leadership in higher education.* Johns Hopkins University Press.

Rodriguez, O., Mejia, M. C., & Johnson, H. (2016). *Determining college readiness in California's community colleges: A survey of assessment and placement policies.* Sacramento: Public Policy Institute of California.

Yeado, J., Haycock, K., Johnstone, R., & Chaplot, P. (2014). *Higher education practice guide: Learning from high-performing and fast-gaining institutions.* Education Trust. http://edtrust.org/resource/education-trust-higher-education-practice-guide-learning-from-high-performing-and-fast-gaining-institutions/

Zimpher, N. L. (2013). Systemness: Unpacking the value of higher education systems. In J. E. Lane & D. B. Johnstone (Eds.), *Higher education systems 3.0: Harnessing systemness, delivering performance* (pp. 27–44). State University of New York Press.

9

NAVIGATING THE MESSY BUSINESS OF MULTICAMPUS SYSTEM CHANGE IN HIGHER EDUCATION

A Framework for Implementation

JASON E. LANE AND
JONATHAN S. GAGLIARDI

ABSTRACT

This chapter presents the innovation cube, a multisided approach to navigate large-scale change in higher education multicampus systems. Distilled from the case studies presented in this volume as well as research on organizational change, the cube discusses three fundamental elements that system leaders need to consider in advancing multicampus change efforts: strategy, structure, and capacity building.

Higher education systems were established for a bygone area, one in which there was a relatively stable resource environment and strong public support for higher education as a public good, most students were "traditional," and the competitive pressures on institutions were not as intense as they are now. Their role was largely as a buffer between politics and academia, shepherding communications, resources, and accountability requirements between the two worlds (Lee & Bowen, 1971). However, over the last 50 years, resources have become increasingly unstable and the costs of public higher education shifted from states to students. The student body is increasingly diverse, underprepared to take on postsecondary education studies, and less likely to attend a single institution throughout their college experience. Elected officials and the media, once largely deferential to higher education, now question its value on a regular basis. These changes have set the stage for higher education systems to reinvent themselves as agents of student success, economic development, and community preservation rather than bureaucracies that protect status quo.

In response to this marked environmental shift, a handful of higher education system leaders have sought to change the role of their systems, seeking to move them from a focus on allocation, coordination, and regulation to instead serve as engines of collaboration—working to harness the collective power of multiple campuses in order to improve student success, strengthen communities, and build state economies (Lane & Johnstone, 2013). Yet change does not come easily, and the higher education community has drawn criticism for its slow response to a rapidly evolving environment. Indeed, many of the bureaucratic and political structures created by and for systems over the last five decades remain intact and serve as impediments to change (McGuiness, 2013).

Some might argue that these historic structures stagnated the United States' postsecondary educational attainment, leading the nation to fall from the most well-educated country in the world 50 years ago to the tenth most well educated in 2018.[1] As noted throughout this volume, even a national goal to increase completion backed by the White House and major private foundations has not precipitously altered the national college completion rate or the overall number of students receiving a high-quality education credential. The reasons are many and the challenges multi-dimensional. Students now navigate between multiple majors and campuses, struggling at times to cobble together the credits they need to unlock the full benefits of a college degree. Student data are isolated and paint an incomplete portrait of how students actually experience higher education (Gagliardi et al., 2018; Lane, 2018). State support has largely stagnated, and there is shrinking support for raising tuition and fees, particularly at a time when wealth and income stratification have made it harder than ever for students to invest in their futures. Global and local competition is on the rise as more countries invest in higher education (Gagliardi, 2015; Lane, 2012; Lane et al., 2015). New technology and the rise of alternative credentials (e.g., badges) threaten to disrupt the credential monopoly long enjoyed by colleges and universities.

Despite these challenges, change in the academy is occurring—but the success is pocketed and the impact mostly on the margins. There are evidence-based strategies that have proven to positively affect, for example, student retention, persistence, and completion (e.g., reforming math pathways, implementing high-impact practices, and using predictive analytics in advising efforts) (see chapter 8). The problem is that much of this activity is focused on isolated impact, and scaling efforts remain largely negligible. For example, at a recent symposium on undergraduate research attend by one of us, the focus was on scaling a particular intervention on intensive writing from one course to five courses. While such effort might be useful for 50 students, it will hardly move the needle on national attainment numbers. The real challenge is to systematically scale up and scale out evidence-based interventions across campuses, systems, and entire states.

The contributors in this volume offer insight into how such scaling efforts are possible, including all the messiness and murkiness along the way. In an environment where isolated impact is king and institutional autonomy is believed to be sacrosanct, it can be incredibly difficult to replicate and scale even the most successful of activities. But the efforts of an increasing number of multicampus system leaders is proving that collaboration is possible, and scaling successful interventions can have large-scale impact on students and communities.

Lest we be accused of having a Pollyannish view of this work, it is important to note that some of the efforts described in this volume have been subject to multiple challenges, including political restructuring, loss of champions, withdrawal of funding, and changing organizational goals. Some of the work has continued despite these challenges; others have been entirely scrapped. The lesson in this work, however, is not the success of any given project. Rather, collectively, these case studies represent a fundamental shift in how multicampus systems approach their work. These early adopters represent in many ways a shifting of the system dynamic—away from that of allocator, regulator, and coordinator to that of facilitator, convener, and incentivizer.

Indeed, in each of the systems involved in this volume (and many others), there is current evidence of how systemness has taken hold and transformed the work of system administrations and their relationship with the campuses. In Maryland, for example, the Kirwan Center for Academic Innovation has continued to lead new collaborative efforts from math redesign to open educational resources. While the Tennessee Board of Regents was significantly reorganized and many staff departed, the system continues to advance its use of data-informed decision-making to support student success across campuses. And while the University of Texas System's Institute for Transformational Learning no longer is in operation, the UT System continues to advance systemwide collaborative approaches such as transfer pathways and new initiatives to address equity challenges. In fact, as detailed in chapter 8, 23 systems now work together with the Taking Student Success to Scale (TS3) initiative to support each other in harnessing their systemness to move the dial on student success and completion. The fundamental idea is that what is discussed in this volume represents the leading edge of change in higher education systems that continues to advance. This final chapter is intended to be a tool kit for those interested in learning from these examples and wanting to implement large-scale change across higher education systems. We distill what is known from research and learned across case studies in this volume into a guide to help others map out a strategy and provide tools to assist with implementation.

LEADING SYSTEMS AS NATURALLY NETWORKED ORGANIZATIONS

Executing system-level change necessitates understanding the dynamics between systems and campuses. Too often conflict arises when systems and campuses fight over the line where campus autonomy stops and system authority begins. In some cases, this tension is inevitable, such as when systems execute their authority to determine which campuses are able to offer which academic programs, leading to system administration telling some campuses they cannot offer everything they want. However, when a system leader sees his or her role as the same as the campus CEO, the conflict can become all-consuming and debilitating. In such situations, it becomes very difficult to develop healthy and productive relationships between the campus and the system administration. Instead, each blames the other for interfering with progress, argues that its way is the right way, and fails to see where collaboration can advance their collective interests.

We believe that effective system leaders realize that systems, when possible, do not compete with institutions for the same domains of authority: they complement them. Rather, they pursue activities and functions that are cross-cutting and supportive of campus missions. Figure 9.1 provides an illustration of how an effective system and campus relationship might be visualized. Instead of seeing campuses and systems along the same axis and determining a line of demarcation between them, we suggest that campuses should

Figure 9.1. Systems as Natural Networked Organizations

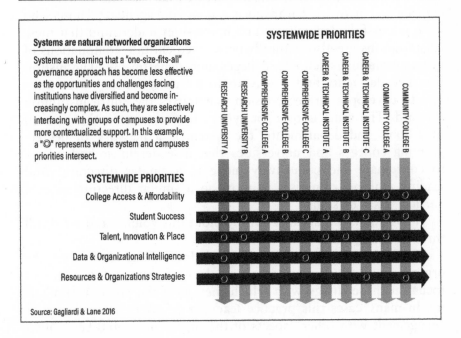

Source: Gagliardi & Lane 2016

operate along one axis and systems operate along another axis. Inevitably, there is overlap, and this is where large-scale change can occur. But the idea is to create collaborative environments that collectively advance student success across all campuses. Therein lies the power of higher education systems.

As discussed throughout this volume, systems have a different position and perspective than campuses. For example, where college leaders tend to focus on the success of students attending their institution, systems take a more holistic view of ensuring students' success as they move within *and between* campuses. By their very nature, systems have the opportunity to leverage resources from across multiple campuses to advance systemwide priorities or to leverage economies of scale through shared services, purchasing arrangements, and negotiated contracts to create cost savings that can be reinvested in student success (or other operational priorities). Such economies of scale do not exist for most institutions—particularly those with smaller or medium-size enrollments—but naturally exist where there are multiple campuses and a formal system governance and administration structure to optimize them.

Moving systems in this direction requires leaders who have a set of characteristics that allows them to harness the power of a coordinated network to advance a common agenda.[2] Those who have successfully led colleges and universities understand that these organizations are also naturally networked entities, compilations of quasi-autonomous schools, colleges, and departments. The institutional leader must find a way to foster unity among these units and to develop a strategic vision that moves the entire institution forward. The same is true for system leaders, except that instead of schools and departments, the system is a network of degree-granting colleges and universities that a leader must find a way to coordinate and collectively move in a similar direction. And leading multiple campuses to move in a similar direction takes a particular set of skills.

Those skills are discussed throughout this volume and we distill three of them here:

1. *Taking a "systems" perspective.* Individuals tend to see the organizations they lead through the lens of their experiences and focus on those things with which they have the greatest familiarity. In many cases this practice leads to a lack of attention to or engagement with other aspects of the organization and certainly a

lack of collective action in addressing issues or pursuing strategic priorities. Within higher education institutions, it is not uncommon for institutional leaders to view their role through the lens of their discipline (if an academic) or their administrative path (e.g., student affairs, finance, government relations). Those who are the most successful tend to set aside the draw of the familiar, to learn about and engage all aspects of their organization. A similar phenomenon is true for system leaders, some of whom may come from a particular institution type (e.g., community college, comprehensive college, or research university), from elsewhere in state government, or from business or industry. In all cases, the system leader needs to learn about the entire system, not just the parts that are familiar or require immediate attention. Only after understanding the disparate parts can one seek to leverage the collective assets of the system.

On the flip side, experienced system leaders understand that their role provides a different perspective or "perch" from which to view higher education. Working across multiple campuses enables leaders to better see higher education as an ecosystem and the constituent campuses as intersecting institutions, often with complementary opportunities and challenges that can frequently more effectively be addressed through collaborative engagements than through isolated activities.

For example, the lens through which a system leader views transfer is often very different than that of the institutional leader. While the institutional leader may consider how to address a student's academic experience while attending the institution, there has often been little an institutional leader can do about the pre- or post-experiences. A system leader, however, is uniquely situated to see transfer from a more holistic perspective and at times has the ability to leverage his or her position to create policy and frameworks that can support the entire student experience, not just the portion limited to a single institution (Lane, et al, 2021).

2. Engaging in facilitative leadership. When trying to foster change, one inevitably gets pushback. In some cases, pushback is a healthy expression of organizational stability that can help leaders avoid potentially hazardous decisions. In other cases, that pushback can be based on assumptions about the way in which things must be done and comes from a place of distrust and fear of the unknown. Very often, when pushed, individuals are unable to provide formal policy that supports their decisions or beliefs, but oral history and culture can be powerful deterrents to change. Similarly, leaders must also possess self-awareness and the ability to confront their own assumptions about how the world operates—challenging themselves to see how things may be done differently or better. The chapters in this book illustrate how challenging the status quo can bring about important change that can positively impact student success.

For example, in chapter 4, Hank Huckaby, former chancellor of the University System of Georgia, challenged leaders in his system to fearlessly explore the future because "we don't know what lies beyond." This challenge led to a new vision for the system, "invent the beyond," which led to the creation of new learning platforms that transformed educational delivery in the state.

System leaders should also be prepared to engage in conversations with system staff members and institutional leaders in which they invite each other to reflect on their role within the system, particularly in terms of how they view their relationship with the "other" (i.e., campus or system). If their view of the other is adversarial, that perspective needs to be understood, unpacked, and challenged, but such exploration can only be done through discussion and dialogue.

One of the most critical roles of the system leader is the ability to convene stakeholders and to frame dialogue. This facilitative leadership role focuses on bringing people together to collectively work toward advancing key goals, such as college completion. Such collaboration could occur through the creation of role-alike groups wherein individuals with similar positions work together to share and address issues of similar interest. More focused task forces, committees, work groups, and so forth can also be created to develop and implement plans designed to address specific goals, such as increasing shared services among campuses, supporting online learning, or advancing supports for diversity, equity, and inclusion.

While system leaders may have the ability to enact policy by exercising whatever governance authority they may have, the reality is that fiats often equate to failure.

Taking a more facilitative role toward leadership can also create more plans that may be more nuanced for the needs of particular campuses and ensure the that change efforts are sustained over time. It also improves the odds of leadership continuity at the uppermost levels, which increases the chances of positive and impactful evolution.

3. *Fostering a collaborative mindset and changing mindsets.* Two matters of perception that stand among the largest challenges facing system leaders: finding ways for campuses to see themselves as part of a system where collective and individual impacts are seen and prioritized equally, and shifting the perception of systems from an unnecessary bureaucratic structure to the glue that holds things together. As described in the preceding chapters, some system leaders are now positioning systems to be viewed as adding value to their constituent campuses, such as by setting a collective vision for the future that all campuses can use as a goal for moving forward.

Effective system leaders create a unified and aspirational vision by leveraging the ability to convene critical stakeholders, aligning the interests of campuses, creating spaces for contextualized innovation by building frameworks of excellence that can be shaped by campuses, and incentivizing innovations among pockets of campuses with converged interests and complementary assets (Gagliardi et al., 2015). In addition to their own reinvention, systems are facilitating innovation at the campus level, scaling out promising practices that have proven effective at a given campus. Examples are Maryland's efforts to work with campuses to redesign math pathways to transform critical gateway courses to support more students in meeting the learning outcomes necessary to be successful in college (see chapter 7) and CSU's efforts to scale high-impact practices (see chapter 3). The additional task of nurturing a shared view of the future can be difficult given historic tensions between systems and campuses that have ignited as a result of social, political, and technological change and financial austerity and distress. However, effective leaders seek to overcome these barriers by facilitating diffused leadership, networked improvement communities, and the process of being the best at getting better.

KEY AREAS OF SYSTEM CHANGE: UNPACKING THE INNOVATION CUBE

Facilitating innovation across systems and campuses has abstract and practical implications and represents a messy, conflictual, and multidimensional challenge. Historically, systems often used hard levers to try to force change—changing policy, adjusting campus funding, and exerting authority to seek to implement change. Many leaders in systems may still be able to recall particularly difficult battles over change when the system attempted (sometimes successfully, sometimes not) to simply force its will on its campuses. These events still occur, and are sometimes necessary, but the chapters in this volume suggest that there are softer levers that, when accompanied by hard levers, are more likely to facilitate meaningful and lasting change. For example, in chapter 5, Denley explores how the Tennessee Board of Regents shifted from an accountability focus to providing resources for and supporting campus-level innovation. In fact, effective system leaders recognize that they cannot alone effect change and impose compliance. Rather, they need to put in place conditions that allow others to embrace a shared vision for change and to innovate.

Moving forward and sustaining an innovation requires leaders to make changes in a variety of areas from recruitment practices to resource strategy to data collection. These areas constitute what we have labeled the "innovation cube," a three-dimensional representation of the interacting areas on which leaders can focus to implement and sustain change (see figure 9.2). There are three primary categories, each represented by its own side of the cube: strategic, structural, and capacity building. Within each of the three areas or sides, there are four squares that a leader may target to create the conditions to facilitate growth of innovation.

The cube is used to illustrate that these functions are not silos. Instead, they are interconnected, functional foci that need to be understood and adjusted in the context of what is happening in the other areas. In fact, the illustration is best viewed as a sort of Rubik's cube, where squares can be moved and manipulated so that each comes in contact with others at some point. Twelve areas of focus may seem a bit overwhelming; however, we believe it is important to identify smaller, more manageable areas to help leaders focus their efforts. Not all areas need to be attended to at once, though it is helpful for leaders to work on at least one area on each side of the cube at the same time.

Following, we describe each of the 12 areas. We have purposefully kept the descriptions short so that readers can more easily digest and process the entirety of the cube in a single sitting. It is important to note that the inevitable tradeoff of shorter descriptions

Figure 9.2. Higher Education Innovation Cube

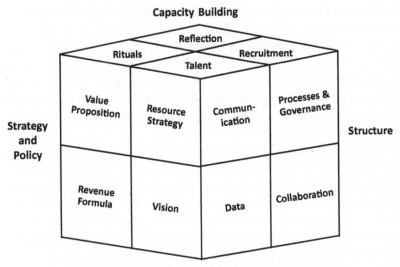

is that all relevant information could not be included, and we encourage readers to explore these topics through additional readings.

For those who are looking for a quick approach to implementing innovation, they will likely not find the easy answers here. Innovation is messy, and sustaining it requires careful attention to different aspects of the system or the institution. We attempt to visualize this fact in figure 9.2. The cube's sides represent three primary areas of focus identified in the case studies in this volume. (We also acknowledge that we present three sides of a cube. The cube is both graphically easier to display and allows for additional sides to be explored through additional research.) Not all chapters in this volume used all areas, and not all successful innovation requires change in each of the squares. However, we believe that the more squares that are addressed, the more likely the innovation will stick.

The Strategic Side

Fostering an environment that embraces innovation requires changes in strategy and policy. Strategy and policy are the more big-picture elements of any change process and are probably the most critical and the most cited in this volume.

Vision. The single most important square on this cube is vision. Innovation is not possible unless leaders have a clear vision for the future that staff can understand and see themselves a part of. It is important for leaders to provide their organization with a clear idea of what they see as its destination. Vision can also inspire others to keep moving forward with change efforts, and if they have a sense of a positive destination, they are more likely to work through obstacles.

Value proposition. Higher education is under fire for its perceived lack of value. Government, the private sector, and civil society are reevaluating the contributions of higher education institutions. As graduation rates remain stagnant and equity gaps persist—and in some cases, even widen for the students who could gain the most from the benefits of a higher education—various stakeholders are questioning whether to continue to invest and rely on the current business model of higher education. System leaders must learn to articulate higher education's value in two directions. System heads are uniquely poised to articulate the broad value of higher education as a public good that can advance the needs of their state. A system leader has multiple campuses under his or her purview, ranging from two campuses in the Southern Illinois University System to 113 in the California Community College System. After the Great Recession in 2008, the State University of New York (SUNY) rallied around the phrase "The Power of SUNY" to communicate the value of SUNY as an economic engine vital to New York's economic turnaround. This same phrase became an important internal message as well. Because campuses often see systems as drains on their own resources, there is also a need to articulate the value proposition of the system administration to the campuses. For the systems discussed in this volume, the value of the systems is that through facilitating and enabling collective action, the system enables campuses to do things they might not otherwise be able to do.

Resource strategy. Higher education leaders need to rethink existing resource strategies to align with this new environment. In this responsibility, system leaders have an advantage over institution leaders because systems tend to have a broader perspective and more opportunity to leverage economies of scale. Rather than simply thinking about how to expand resource bases, higher education leaders at all levels need to consider how to conserve and strategically reallocate existing funding. Institutions need to ask difficult questions about what to fund and, more critically, what not to fund. Collaboration will become more important, not just through sharing of back-office functions like purchasing and IT contracts, but also through thinking about ways to align resources from multiple institutions to build joint-degree programs, launch student success initiatives, and build seamless matriculation pipelines between multiple campuses.

Revenue formula. This discussion points to a more surgical approach to enterprise management that is dependent on student access and success and cost and affordability. Systems developed in a time when the basic financial model of higher education was best described as a cost spiral: the desire of colleges and universities to spend everything they have, such that if revenues increase, costs do, too (Bowen, 1980). Others more recently have also noted that higher education has an insatiable appetite for new resources, further spiraling up costs. These tendencies led Ehrenberg (2002) to label higher education institutions as "cookie monsters" that search for all the resources they can find and then gobble them up, and Bok (2003) has gone further to call them "compulsive gamblers," with desires that always extend beyond their resources. However, since those writings, resource streams have become increasingly strained with state support stagnating and the national student debt crisis putting the brakes on years of significant tuition increases.

In earlier resource-stable environments, there was little necessity for innovation, and that which did occur often existed at the edges and was paid for by new resources. In a resource-constrained and unstable environment, higher education campuses and systems need to consider new ways of reducing costs and reallocating existing resources to evidence-based, high-impact activities. Many academic leaders are now forced to evaluate the returns on their investments, examining impact on student success as well as the number of students impacted. Indeed, even some high-impact programs may need to be curtailed or eliminated if their effects only reach a few students. This notion of return on investment can be controversial in organizations that are used to expanding and not contracting, and which have been culturally averse to integrating a revenue-minded manner of operation. But when resources are limited, new investment may have to come from reallocation of existing dollars. Hereto, the economy of scale of a system can be beneficial to identify cost savings and strategic reinvestments. As an example, in 2011, SUNY initiated a systemwide shared services initiative to identify where collaboration could reduce expenses so that new resources could be freed up to be reinvested in direct educational and student support activities. Through a process that brought together campus and system staff, a plan was developed to scale internal expertise, reduce reliance on external vendors (when appropriate), and develop shared procurement efforts. Within five years, the program had yielded more than $100 million in funds to be reinvested in student success efforts (Zimpher, 2016). The benefits yielded by campuses was only possible because of the coordination with other campuses in the system and the system's ability to both convene critical stakeholders and to develop and implement a plan.

All of this means that large-scale change may necessitate a rethinking of the fundamental revenue strategies that have served higher education in the last 50 years.

The Structural Side

Areas with the most tension between systems and campuses include tenure policies, academic program approval (or disapproval), budget allocations, enrollment strategies, data governance and stewardship, and back-office functions. In many cases, the discourse devolves around issues of the apportionment of authority and autonomy—who gets to be in control. Inevitably, these debates lead to campuses chaffing about new mandates and edicts, especially when the system imposes them via a top-down, mandate-centered approach that looks less like a collaborative, strategic approach and feels more like a punishment. As we found in this volume, some systems are doing a better job at engaging campuses in the change efforts, delivering a more compelling message, and being more strategic about the end goal. This is particularly the case when the focus is on improving student success, which can (and should) be a shared goal of campuses. Below are key structural approaches to advancing change within systems.

Collaboration. Structures and processes to facilitate collaboration are critical for meaningful and sustainable system-level change. Unless campuses (or other units) are willing to collaborate toward achieving a greater goal (e.g., seamless transfer, closing achievement gaps), widespread innovation is unlikely to occur. In fact, it is the historic push toward autonomy and isolated impact that gave rise to the cases in the book—a desire to break down barriers and to scale interventions that work to support success. System leaders need to develop environments that are conducive and encouraging of inter-campus collaboration. This work may include role-alike groups, special task forces, or systemwide convenings that bring people together to work toward achievement of larger initiatives or visions.

Data. We all say that we like to use data, but not everyone actually does. In many cases, it is not because we dislike using data; instead, the data we need do not exist or do not exist either in the format we need the data or because the data owner does not want to share the information. Data integration is increasingly vital. We need less topically stove-piped data that bridge departments and administrative functions, and institutions and systems, to foster decision analytics that improve the health of our organizations (Gagliardi & Wellman, 2015; Gagliardi, 2018). We prefer doctors to have as much data as possible when advising on patients' health; yet the same expectation does not seem to exist for advising on students' education. Identifying ways to aggregate data, even if decision makers just look at basic ratios of cost to completion or efficiency of space, are woefully absent and have yet to envelop entire campuses let alone decisions. Whether using evidence to create policy or policy to create evidence, we need data that are timely, accurate, relevant, and which focus more on actionable insight rather than simply on statistical significance.

Process and governance. Within the academic environment, how things are achieved can be as important as the outcome. In short, process matters. Sustainable success is largely contingent on the engagement of a broad range of stakeholders—students, faculty, staff, presidents, and trustees. Yet system offices (and their leaders) often exist apart from the campus setting. The same structures of shared governance that enable broad stakeholder engagement may not exist at the system level. Therefore, it is important for system leaders to be aware of the need to develop processes and governance mechanisms to ensure multiple voices help inform policy and practice and can, in turn, help champion the work on the campus. Regular involvement with the campus president and provosts is a necessity as they will set the tone for change and the system relationship on their campus.

It is also important to bring in the voice of faculty and students. A defining contribution of the academy is the notion of shared governance, which should be seen as a tool to be leveraged, not ignored. Within the campus setting, a standard governance model is the existence of committees and an academic senate that give voice to the faculty and are responsible for working with the administration to move the institution forward. Yet such structures do not always exist at the system level. Some systems, such as CUNY and SUNY, have systemwide faculty governing bodies that regularly engage with system leadership and bring the voice of the faculty. Some systems, including the State University System of Florida and the Tennessee Board of Regents, have mandated faculty representation as part of the composition of their governing board. System heads may also choose to include students and faculty in their cabinet or other administrative bodies to ensure their voices are part of system planning and dialogue.

Communication. Communication can be a difficult act on a college campus. The difficulty is amplified significantly at the system level. Innovation and change require clear and constant communication with all stakeholders. Messaging has to be focused and easily understandable and multiple communication channels need to be leveraged. If you think you have communicated enough, you probably have not. Within SUNY, we thought that academic information shared with presidents would then be shared with their provosts. At a meeting of provosts, we learned this was not the case. As a result, we started to send official correspondence to multiple groups—almost always to the attention of presidents, but with copies to all relevant stakeholders on the campus so that we did not need to rely on a narrow communication chain.

In addition, it is important to create mutually reinforcing communication patterns. Strategic initiatives should be made part of regular meetings and correspondence, so that the importance of the initiative is consistently reinforced. For example, reporting mechanisms should include data that relate to the initiatives. Reports to the governing board should include updates on the initiatives. Meetings of presidents and other senior campus officials should incorporate updates and when possible meaningful discussion and dialogue. Who carries the message can also be important and having campus leaders serve as champions and message carriers can be particularly effective in relating to other campus staff.

The Capacity Building Side

Building human capacity to implement innovation is probably one of the most overlooked aspects of this process. If faculty and staff do not have the knowledge, skills, or interests to adopt and embrace an innovation, it will never take hold regardless of how great the vision, how much money is invested, or how structures are changed.

A timely example comes from the current turn toward data analytics on many campuses. As discussed in chapter 5, the use of data analytics in systems such as the Tennessee Board of Regents has proven to have significant impact on student retention and success. Consequently, institutions and systems have rushed to implement their own data analytics interventions, usually focused on using data to better inform advising and to more quickly identify potentially at-risk students. The problem is that no matter how much money an institution dumps into developing or buying an analytics solution, the impact will be minimal if the human capacity to use these tools is not built.

The following four areas are helpful to build an organization's human capacity to embrace and implement innovation.

Recruitment. The first time many employees learn about an organization is during the recruitment phase. How the job description is written, whom candidates meet, and how they are treated serve to form their initial impression of the organization and the direction in which it is headed. Hiring the right people is the first step toward making sure the right team is in place. Within systems, the most important hires are the campus presidents, as they are the individuals who set the overall tone and direction on their campus. Facilitating systemwide change requires the support of these individuals; without it, it is difficult to bring their campus along. When the University of Illinois System was recently working to create a more collaborative environment between its flagship campus and the system office, it designated that the chancellor of the Urbana–Champaign campuses was also the vice president of the system. The signal was clear: The person in this role needed to understand that he or she was both a leader of the campus and part of the system's leadership team. A dual appointment is not the only way to convey this message, however. SUNY altered its presidential search process to include language in the job description, interview questions, and meetings with system staff to send a similar message to candidates. Again, the message is simple: If you are not interested in being a team player in a system, SUNY would not be the place for you.

Professional development. Change is not possible without the right team in place. Recruitment is a critical part of creating that team, but for many leaders, the majority of their team is incumbent staff. Professional development therefore comes into play. As previously described, implementation of innovation requires development of individuals in the organization, providing them with both the knowledge and skills needed to be successful. For example, when SUNY sought to scale a new math remediation program (the Carnegie Foundation's Quantway program) across its 30 community colleges, the system knew that a mandate approach would not work. Even though the evidence showed that students in sections that used the Quantway approach succeeded at three times the rate of students in other sections, large-scale implementation required faculty education regarding the potential impact of the new curriculum and the building of skills to teach it. Thus, the bulk of the implementation effort was placed in providing professional development opportunities for the faculty who taught math remediation. The impact was quick and meaningful. Since they were educated about the impact and provided with the skills to implement the innovative new curriculum, not only did they embrace the change but they often also became champions of it on their own campus. Even some of the most vocal critics became the innovation's most ardent supporters because of the professional development opportunity. While systems and institutions are increasingly willing to invest in new technological and curricular solutions, professional development opportunities related to these innovations seem to be neglected. However, without professional development, innovation will fail.

Rituals. A ritual is a routinized symbolic act that "usually has a statable purpose, but one that invariably alludes to more than it says, and has many meanings at once" (Moore & Meyerhoff, 1977, p. 5). Rituals, as well as a host of other symbolic aspects of an organization (e.g., ceremonies, stories, and values), are often overlooked when a leader considers change. Building the capacity of a team requires an understanding of the symbolic elements of the organization and determining how to co-opt them to support innovation (instead of blocking it).

Reflection. The value of experience is what can be learned, and learning requires reflection. Reflection first requires one to look inward to understand how an experience or a set of experiences shape one's view of the world and those with whom we interact. Second, we must look at how our actions affect others. This experience allows us to deconstruct who we are as a leader and to better understand how we lead and how we can improve ourselves as leaders. There is a natural tendency to claim credit for those things that are successful and assign blame to others for those that are not. The reality is often much messier. Our successes are often the result of the work of many as are our failures—and leaders need to recognize their roles in both. Innovation requires that leaders be willing to reflect and to use what is learned in that reflection to advance change and new ideas. Effective system leaders create environments and structures that seek feedback, support reflection, and allow for making adjustments in strategy and process.

ORGANIZATIONAL CULTURE

It is important to note that organizational culture is not specifically included in the innovation cube. There is a widely quoted maxim that "culture beats strategy," and we have all probably seen examples of this phenomenon, particularly in culture-steeped higher education institutions. Authors in this volume have talked about the need to change institution and system cultures. However, for as much as culture matters, it is incredibly difficult to identify what exactly culture is, let alone change it. Therefore, it does not have its own square. Its omission from the cube does not mean that culture is unimportant—quite the contrary. Making changes in each of these squares will lead to changes in the organizational culture. The language used in the hiring process sets the tone of what is expected of new hires. Adjusting the resource strategy shifts individual rewards. Shifting the value proposition alters how we think about the goals of the institution. Collectively, these actions work toward fostering change in organizational culture.

Of course, this approach represents a fundamental departure from the way things have been done for a very long time, creating natural tensions and conflict. Gone are the days when institutions could act in isolation, and systems could take a passive role in steering them collectively. Institutions and systems are facing the reality that to thrive they must change, and in many cases, it is not because of self-reflection. They are being told that change must happen by stakeholders who acknowledge past success but demand better performance in the future. It is a difficult task to confront, and it causes institutions and systems to lash out at one another, even if they are increasingly dependent on one another.

BACKBONE SUPPORT

In all the examples included in this volume, a common theme is the inclusion of some form of backbone support. This backbone has responsibility for moving the innovation effort forward. This entity is not necessarily responsible for providing the vision or leadership of the innovation, rather it is the one responsible for ensuring the effort moves forward by convening the right people, tracking data and progress, creating communication patterns, and so forth. This backbone can be an office, a team, a committee, or something else, but it has to have a formal charge and authority for advancing the innovation effort. While it might not have direct reporting lines to the system leader, it should have access to the system leader.

ADVANCING SYSTEMNESS

Systems and campuses are changing to meet unprecedented demands to improve student outcomes, reduce costs, increase efficiencies, and demonstrate return on investment in ways big and small. It makes sense: As fewer and fewer students stay in one place, and as we continue to grow into a more networked and globalized society, systems are an imperfect but effective solution. Evidenced by the contributions to this volume, emergent foci on predictive analytics and evidence-based practices, course and curricular pathway redesign, high-impact practices, student mobility and transfer, customized technology-enhanced courses and degree pathways, teacher preparation, and the cradle-to-career pipeline are all underway. The success of these efforts is owed to the emerging system roles of implementation and planning, as well as scaling out what has been scaled up. These new roles and ongoing organizational transformations focused on improving student outcomes are a direct result of these silent innovators we know as higher education systems.

The case studies in this volume illustrate how some early adopters of the systemness concept sought to bring together stakeholders from across their campuses to work together to create change. The historic structures of systems have not been attuned toward such collaborative arrangements. However, some innovative system leaders have worked to leverage these structures in new ways—to better respond to the challenges now confronting higher education—and, in many ways, they are among those most well situated to move the dial on completion. As we discussed, first, these leaders have a unique "perch" that allows them to see a larger higher education ecosystem and to affect change that can positively affect student success across multiple institutions. Second, they engage in facilitative leadership that is people-centered and focused on goal attainment. Finally, they foster collaborative mindsets, supporting system and campus leaders in seeing the value of working together toward a greater good rather than competing with each other over finite resources. In many ways, system heads are similar to admirals of a fleet, harnessing the collective impact of their ships (i.e., campuses) to work toward achieving a greater goal that no single entity can achieve. As Nancy Zimpher comments in her preface, the vision of systemness is that the whole is greater than the sum of the parts.

CHAPTER 9 TAKEAWAYS

- Systems are naturally networked organizations that can facilitate cross-campus collaborations.

- Systems have multiple tools at their disposal, ranging from the ability to convene key stakeholders to creating an enabling policy environment that supports change.

- The chapter describes the innovation cube as a metaphor representing the ways in which systems can foster change.

- The three sides of the cube are strategic, structural, and capacity building. Each of these areas have four foci to help guide innovation efforts.

NOTES

1. According to the Organisation for Economic Co-operation and Development (OECD 2020), the United States had the tenth highest percentage of 25–34-year-olds with a tertiary education (49.4%) in 2018. Tertiary education is defined by the OECD as "having completed the highest level of education, by age group. This includes both theoretical programmes leading to advanced research or high skill professions such as medicine and more vocational programmes leading to the labour market."

2. Educational organizations, including systems, have characteristics of loose coupling, in that there tend to be limited internal controls, increased decentralization of authority, and departments within an organization are minimally confederated (Weick, 1976). We have used the termed "naturally networked" in this chapter to focus on the advantages of a system being a network of campuses, rather than on the characteristics that might challenge greater coordination and a move toward systemness.

REFERENCES

Bok, D. (2003). *Universities in the marketplace: The commercialization of higher education.* Princeton University Press.

Bowen, H. R. (1980). *The costs of higher education.* Jossey-Bass.

Ehrenberg, R. G. (2002). *Tuition rising: Why college costs so much.* Harvard University Press.

Gagliardi, J. S. (2015). From perpetuation to innovation: Breaking through barriers to change in higher education. In J. E. Lane (Ed.), *Higher education reconsidered: Executing change to drive collective impact.* State University of New York Press.

Gagliardi, J. S., Martin, R. R., Wise, K., & Blaich, C. (2015). The system effect: Scaling high impact campuses across campuses. *New Directions for Higher Education,* 15–26.

Gagliardi, J. S., Parnell, A., & Carpenter-Hubin, J. (Eds.) (2018). *The analytics revolution.* Stylus.

Gagliardi, J. S., & Wellman, J. (2015). *Meeting demands for improvements in public system institutional research.* National Association of System Heads.

Gagliardi, J. S. (2018). The analytics revolution in higher education. In J. S. Gagliardi, A. Parnell & J. Carpenter-Hubin (Eds.), *The analytics revolution.* Stylus.

Lane, J. E. (2012). Higher education and economic competitiveness. In J. E. Lane & D. B. Johnstone (Eds.), *Universities and colleges as economic drivers: Measuring and building success* (pp. 1–30). State University of New York Press.

Lane, J. E. (2018). Data analytics, systemness and predicting student success in college: Examining how the data revolution matters to higher education policy makers. In J. S. Gagliardi, A. Parnell, & J. Carpenter-Hubin (Eds.), *The analytics revolution.* Stylus.

Lane, J. E., & Johnstone, D. B. (Eds.). (2013). *Higher education systems 3.0: Harnessing systemness, delivering performance.* State University of New York Press.

Lane, J. E., Khan, M., & Knox, D. (2021). *The emerging role of public higher education systems in transfer student success.* National Association of System Heads.

Lane, J. E., Owens, T., & Kinser, K. (2015). *Cross border higher education, international trade, and economic competitiveness.* A policy paper prepared for i-LEAP.

Lee, E. C., & Bowen, F. M. (1971). *The multicampus university*. McGraw-Hill.

McGuiness, A. (2013). History and evolution of higher education systems in the United States. In J. E. Lane & D. B. Johnstone (Eds.), *Higher education systems 3.0: Harnessing systemness, delivering performance* (pp. 45–74). State University of New York Press.

Moore, S. F., & Meyerhoff, B. (1977). *Secular ritual*. Van Gorcum.

Organisation for Economic Co-operation and Development (OECD). (2020). Population with tertiary education (indicator). doi:10.1787/0b8f90e9-en

Weick, K. (1976). Educational organizations as loosely coupled systems. *Administrative Sciences Quarterly, 21,*1–9.

Zimpher, N. L. (2016). State of the University address. https://www.suny.edu/about/leadership/chancellor-nancy-zimpher/speeches/2016-sou/

CONTRIBUTORS

M. J. Bishop is Associate Vice Chancellor and inaugural director of the University System of Maryland's William E. Kirwan Center for Academic Innovation, which was established in 2013 to enhance and promote USM's position as a national leader in higher education academic innovation. The center conducts research on best practices, disseminates findings, offers professional development opportunities for institutional faculty and administrators, and supports the 12 public institutions that are part of the system as they continue to expand innovative academic practices. Prior to coming to USM, Dr. Bishop was Associate Professor and Director of the Lehigh University College of Education's Teaching, Learning, and Technology program where, in addition to being responsible for the institution's graduate programs in instructional technology, she also played a leadership role in guiding the general and special education teacher preparation programs through a curricular overhaul to address the new Pennsylvania Department of Education (PDE) guidelines for teacher certification. While at Lehigh, Dr. Bishop received several awards for her research and teaching, including the 2013 Stabler Award for Excellence in Teaching for leading students to "excellence in their chosen field" as well as "excellence as human beings and as leaders of society."

Joann A. Boughman is Senior Vice Chancellor for Academic and Student Affairs for the 12 institutions in the University System of Maryland, totaling more than 175,000 students and 14,000 faculty. Responsibilities include academic policy, academic planning and accountability, faculty affairs, program evaluation, transfer and articulation issues, academic innovation, cultural diversity, and student affairs, including Title IX and student health and wellness.

Dr. Boughman received her bachelor's and PhD degrees from Indiana University. At the University of Maryland, Baltimore, she has been a professor in the School of Medicine and Dental School, Vice President for Research and Development, Dean of the Graduate School, and Vice President for Academic Affairs. She is currently Adjunct Professor of Medicine, Epidemiology and Preventive Medicine and a professor in the Graduate School. Dr. Boughman served as the CEO of the American Society of Human Genetics for a decade, representing the more than 7,000 geneticist members on policy issues, and provided testimony on Capitol Hill. She is a board-certified medical geneticist and has authored 68 peer-reviewed journal articles, 15 book chapters, and more than 100 abstracts.

Houston D. Davis is the eleventh president of the University of Central Arkansas (UCA). President Davis joined UCA from the University System of Georgia where he served Kennesaw State University as Interim President from June to November 2016 and as Executive Vice Chancellor and Chief Academic Officer of the University System of Georgia from 2012 to 2016. He also previously served as Vice Chancellor for Academic Affairs for the Oklahoma State Regents for Higher Education and functioned as the state's liaison to the national Complete College America initiative. Prior to 2007, he served as Associate Vice Chancellor for Academic Affairs for the Tennessee Board of Regents, on faculty and in academic leadership for Austin Peay State University, in fiscal and academic affairs for the Tennessee Higher Education Commission, and as a regional counselor for the University of Memphis. President Davis is also involved in research projects and writing in higher education governance, economic development and accountability issues, and has served on several national advisory groups on higher education policy, degree completion, academic preparation and accountability. He received his Doctor of Philosophy in education and human development at Vanderbilt University and his Master of Education in educational administration at Tennessee State University. President Davis earned his Bachelor of Science in political science at the University of Memphis.

Tristan Denley currently serves as Executive Vice Chancellor for Academic Affairs and Chief Academic Officer at the University System of Georgia. Before moving to Georgia in May 2017 he served as Vice Chancellor for Academic Affairs at the Tennessee Board of Regents from August 2013 until May 2017 and Vice President for Academic Affairs at Austin Peay State University from January 2009. Originally from Penzance, England, Dr. Denley earned his PhD in mathematics from Trinity College Cambridge and held positions in Sweden, Canada, and the University of Mississippi before coming to Tennessee. At Ole Miss he served as Chair of Mathematics and Senior Fellow of the Residential College program. Throughout his career, he has taken a hands-on approach in a variety of initiatives impacting student success. His most recent work has been to transform developmental education and advising at a system scale. His work continues in using a data-informed approach to implement a wide variety of system-scale initiatives surrounding college completion, stretching from education redesign in a variety of disciplines to the role of predictive analytics and data mining, cognitive psychology, and behavioral economics in higher education.

Jonathan S. Gagliardi is Assistant Vice Chancellor for Academic Innovation and Effectiveness at the City University of New York. Prior to serving in this role, Gagliardi served as Assistant Vice President for Strategy, Policy, and Analytics at Lehman College. He previously served as Associate Director for the American Council on Education's Center for Policy Research and Strategy and as Visiting Fellow for the Rockefeller Institute of Government. Prior to that, Jonathan was a Chancellor's Fellow of the State University of New York (SUNY) system and Deputy Director of the National Association of System Heads. In these roles, Dr. Gagliardi helped create, lead, and implement national completion initiatives aimed at scaling out evidence-based practices that promote student success, including Taking Student Success to Scale. Jonathan is recognized for his expertise in a number of areas, including the evolving use of data analytics in higher education; innovation and organizational transformation; the higher education leadership pipeline; and the intersection of higher education, the workforce, and student success. Dr. Gagliardi holds a PhD in higher education policy and leadership from the University at Albany (SUNY). Most recently, Jonathan co-edited *The Analytics Revolution in Higher Education: Big Data, Organizational Learning, and Student Success* (2018).

Myk Garn is an academic innovator and strategist with over 30 years' experience developing, deploying, and leading college and state system instructional, operational, organizational, policy, and strategic models. Dr. Garn's work provides new prisms and perspectives through which our system and institutional leaders can envision and reimagine our core educational activities. As an educational product strategist, he focuses on new learning models that occur in the opportunity spaces where teaching and learning are catalyzed by technology. He leads the USG Precision Academics initiative, which creates awareness and understanding of how the digital transformation of instruction through data, analytics, competency-paced, adaptive models of learning. His mission and passion are considering what the system is doing now—informing what it needs to do next—and discovering what will come after next.

Audrey Hovannesian holds a bachelor's degree in liberal studies, a master's in education, and an EdD in educational leadership from CSU San Bernardino, where she studied issues related to assessment, psychometric measurement, and practices that increase student success. In higher education she coordinated assessment and student success at the campus level before leading the assessment of high-impact practices in the California State University System. She has served as a research fellow for the Carnegie Project on the Educational Doctorate and currently directs Information Technology, Assessment/Accountability, and Institutional Effectiveness at the Victor Valley Union High School District.

Jason E. Lane serves as Dean of the College of Education, Health, and Society at Miami University in Oxford, Ohio, and Professor of Higher Education and Leadership. Dr. Lane's scholarly expertise focuses on systems leadership and organizational change within higher education, particularly as it relates to the emerging relationship between higher education, policy and politics, and internationalization. He is founding Executive Director of SUNY's Strategic, Academic, and Innovative Leadership (SAIL) Institute, co-leader of the system's Leadership Academy of the National Association of System Heads, and co-director of the Association of Governing Board's Institute for Leadership and Governance. Previous roles include Dean of the

School of Education at the State University of New York at Albany, Senior Associate Vice Chancellor of Academic Planning and Strategic Leadership for the SUNY system, and Deputy Director of the Nelson A. Rockefeller Institute of Government. He has published nearly 100 scholarly papers and more than 10 books, including *Higher Education Systems 3.0: Harnessing Systemness, Delivering Performance* (also from SUNY Press) and *Academic Leadership and Governance in Higher Education* (from Stylus Press).

Rebecca R. Martin is Executive Director of the National Association of System Heads (NASH), an association of chief executives of the college and university systems of public higher education in the United States. NASH has worked hard to form a network of presidents, chancellors, executive directors, and commissioners. Together, this group supports leaders and their peers in the unique roles they play. Rebecca served as Director of Higher Education and Senior Fellow at the Education Delivery Institute (EDI) from 2010 to 2015. Before joining EDI, Rebecca served as Senior Vice President for Academic Affairs for the University of Wisconsin System. Under her leadership, the system expanded the use of high-impact practices and aggressively focused on improving the retention and graduation rates of underserved students. Rebecca served for five years as Provost and Vice Chancellor at the University of Wisconsin Parkside, where she also taught as a tenured professor in political science. Earlier, she served at the University of Vermont and the California State University System. She earned her doctorate in public administration from the University of Southern California, her master's degree in librarianship from San Jose State University, and her bachelor's degree in educational psychology and history from the University of California Santa Cruz.

Steven Mintz is Senior Advisor to the President of Hunter College for Student Success and Strategic Initiatives and Professor of History at the University of Texas at Austin. He previously served as Executive Director of the University of Texas System's Institute for Transformational Learning. The author and editor of 15 books, he writes regularly on curricular and pedagogical innovation for *Inside Higher Ed*'s "Higher Ed Gamma" blog. The past president of H-Net: Humanities and Social Sciences Online and the Society for the History of Children and Youth, he has also chaired the Council on Contemporary Families.

Ken O'Donnell is Vice Provost at California State University Dominguez Hills. He helps lead the division's work on program quality, resource allocation, faculty affairs and development, student success and engagement, and innovation. Ken connects student success efforts and high-impact educational practices across multiple departments and divisions, advancing work to improve our understanding of educational effectiveness, equity, and student engagement. CSU Dominguez Hills is committed to sharing all it discovers in this area, as a national model and laboratory for student success. Before coming to Dominguez Hills, Ken was Senior Director of Student Engagement at the CSU Office of the Chancellor, leading system-wide offices and projects to strengthen STEM education, community engagement, transfer and articulation, and general education, all toward improving learning and persistence and closing achievement gaps. Ken has written about and addressed numerous conferences and workshops around the country on the intersections between deep learning and student success, the benefits of locating college learning in real-world contexts, and the role of public universities in higher education reform. Before coming to CSU Ken was a member of the screenwriting faculty and an assistant dean at the film school at Chapman University. He and his wife Cyndi live in Southern California.

Art Seavey is Director of Evoca Learn, an educational media service working to develop and provide new forms of learning. Previously he served as Senior Program Officer in the United States Program at the Bill & Melinda Gates Foundation, where he led efforts to forecast the structure of the higher education industry and to grow new models for institutions and systems that create more equitable outcomes for low-income students and students of color. Before that, Art was Director of Policy and Partnership Development for the University System of Georgia, where he supported the vice chancellor for educational access and success in efforts to envision, implement, and resource strategic partnerships inside and outside the system to improve performance. Seavey received his Bachelor of Science from the Georgia Institute of Technology and his Master of Public Policy from Duke University.

Nancy L. Zimpher is among the most in-demand thought leaders in higher education in the United States and around the world. From 2009 to 2017, Zimpher served as the 12th chancellor of the State University of New York, the nation's largest comprehensive system of public higher education. Prior to SUNY, she served as President of the University of Cincinnati, Chancellor of the University of Wisconsin Milwaukee, and Executive Dean of the Professional Colleges and Dean of the College of Education at The Ohio State University. Zimpher is co-founder and current chair of StriveTogether, a national network of innovative partnerships that holistically address challenges across the education pipeline. Concurrent with her role as SUNY chancellor, she served as chair of the National Association of System Heads from 2014 to 2017, was on the Board of Governors of the New York Academy of Sciences from 2011 to 2016 and CEOs for Cities from 2012 to 2013, and led the national Coalition of Urban Serving Universities from 2005 to 2011.

Index

Note: Page numbers in *italics* indicate figures; those with a *t* indicate tables.